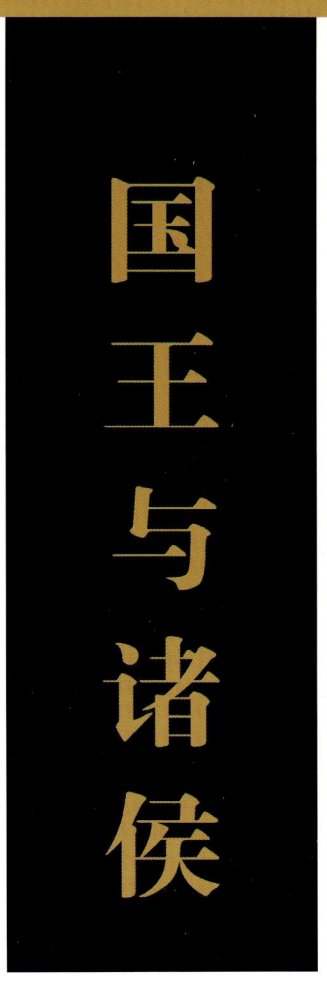

中国河南青铜文明展
KINGS AND MARQUISES
EXHIBITION OF ANCIENT BRONZE CIVILIZATION OF HENAN, CHINA

河南省文物局 主编

中州古籍出版社

图书在版编目（CIP）数据

国王与诸侯：中国河南青铜文明 / 河南省文物局编. —— 郑州：中州古籍出版社，2013.3
ISBN 978-7-5348-4173-6

Ⅰ．①国… Ⅱ．①洛… Ⅲ．①青铜器（考古）－研究－河南省－三代时期 Ⅳ．①K876.414

中国版本图书馆CIP数据核字(2013)第048408号

责任编辑：王小方　周媛

责任校对：高西省　王军花　赵星汉

出版社：中州古籍出版社

（地址：郑州市经五路66号　邮政编码：450002）

发行单位：新华书店

承印单位：洛阳创彩印刷有限公司

开本：889mm×1194mm　1/16	印张：14
字数：13千字	印数：3000册
版次：2013年3月第1版	印次：2013年3月第1次印刷
书号：ISBN 978-7-5348-4173-6	
定价：280.00元	

本书如有印装质量问题，由承印厂负责调换。

《国王与诸侯 — 中国河南青铜文明展》

主　　编：河南省文物局
主办单位：河南省文物局
承办单位：洛阳市文物管理局
　　　　　洛阳博物馆
协办单位：河南博物院
　　　　　河南省文物考古研究院
　　　　　郑州博物馆
　　　　　安阳博物馆
　　　　　信阳博物馆
　　　　　三门峡市虢国博物馆

编辑委员会

主　　任：陈爱兰
副 主 任：马萧林
　　　　　付玉林
　　　　　刘德胜
编　　委：王献本
　　　　　谢虎军
　　　　　高西省

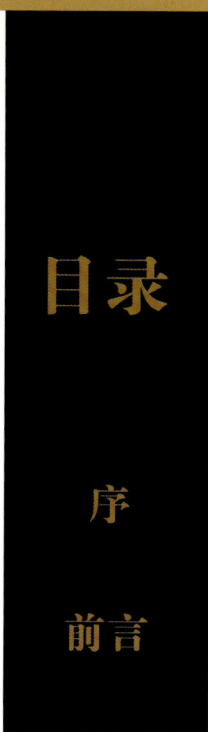

目录

序

前言

第一部分 王国崛起 器以藏礼 夏代

偃师二里头青铜器 ················· *012*

第二部分 神秘王朝 雄奇瑰宝 商代

郑州商城青铜器 ················· *020*

安阳殷墟青铜器 ················· *034*

罗山莽张息国铜器 ················ *050*

第三部分 礼乐大成 赫赫成周 西周时期

洛阳西周王室青铜器 ··· *064*

鹿邑太清宫殷遗民青铜器 ······································· *090*

郑州洼刘舌族青铜器 ··· *116*

平顶山应国贵族青铜器 ··· *124*

三门峡虢国贵族青铜器 ··· *136*

第四部分 群雄逐鹿 异彩纷呈 东周时期

洛阳东周王室青铜器 ··· *156*

新郑郑国青铜器 ·· *168*

淅川楚国青铜器 ·· *180*

淮诸小国青铜器 ·· *192*

结束语

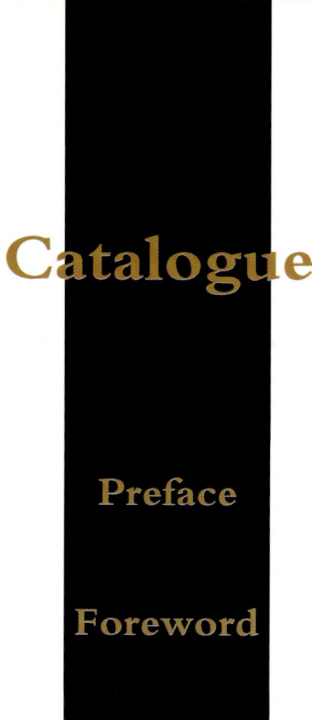

Catalogue

Preface

Foreword

Part I Formation of the state Xia Dynasty

Bronzewares from Erlitou site in Yanshi *012*

Part II The mysterious Dynasty Shang Dynasty

Bronzewares from the capital of the Shang Dynasty in Zhengzhou *020*

Bronzewares from the Yin Ruins in Anyang *034*

Bronzewares from the ancient state "Xi" at Mangzhang in Luoshan *050*

Part III Establishment of the ritual and music system Western Zhou Dynasty

Bronzewares from the royal families of the Western Zhou Dynasty in Luoyang ·················· *064*

Bronzewares from the tomb of the descendants of the Shang Dynasty at Taiqing palace in Luyi ····· *090*

Bronzewares from the ancient familie "She" at Waliu in Zhengzhou ························ *116*

Bronzewares from the noble families of ancient states "Ying" in Pingdingshan ················ *124*

Bronzewares from the noble families of ancient states "Guo" in Shanmenxia ················· *136*

Part IV Fight among rivals for the throne Eastern Zhou Dynasty

Bronzewares from the royal families of the Eastern zhou Dynasty in Luoyang ················· *156*

Bronzewares from the ancient state "Zheng" in Xinzheng ······························· *168*

Bronzewares from the ancient state "Chu" in Xichuang ································ *180*

Bronzewares from ancient states along Huai River ··································· *192*

Conclusion

序

黄河，蜿蜒流动在中国北方，全长约5464公里，流域面积约79.5万平方公里，作为炎黄子孙心中的圣河，这里最早沐浴了文明之光，也是华夏文明的摇篮。河南，因其大部分位于黄河以南而得名。约一万年以前，这里进入新石器时代，先民们逐河而居，享受着大河的富饶，播下文明的火种。新石器时代晚期，黄河流域进入了早期国家确立的重要时期。从夏代到战国两千多年的历史长河里，中原大地王室更迭，诸侯逐鹿，上演了一幕幕惊心动魄的纷争离合，河南也逐渐发展成为华夏文明的中心。数千年来，河南出土的大量精美文物折射出先民生活的百姿，彰显了华夏文明的辉煌。

夏商周三代长达两千年，被称为中国的青铜时代。这一时期，河南也成为许多王室与诸侯定都之地。偃师二里头夏代都城、郑州商代都城、安阳殷墟和洛阳东周王城等都是当时重要的青铜铸造中心。河南出土的大量青铜文物，种类丰富，造型独特，工艺精湛，很大程度上代表了当时中国金属冶铸的先进水平。青铜器因其材质的稀有和工艺的复杂，从诞生的那天起，就注定了它的高贵与神秘，成为王室和诸侯的专属用品和礼仪及等级的象征。此次展览精心挑选出的117件（组）展品，多数为河南近年来的考古新发现，基本涵盖了所有的青铜器物类别，全面展示了这一重要历史时期的社会风貌，体现了黄河流域青铜时代文明的多姿与灿烂。

中国河南与瑞典文化交流源远流长。90多年前瑞典学者安特生先生在河南渑池首次发现并确认"仰韶文化"这一新石器时代文化遗存，开启了双方在文物保护方面合作交流的序幕。近几年来，河南文物部门和瑞典文物博物馆机构开展了广泛合作，中原文化日益为瑞典民众了解和熟悉。特别是2012年8月，河南省文物局与瑞典国立世界文化博物馆签署了5年合作协议，进一步深化拓展在文物保护、考古发掘、科学研究、人才培养、文物展览等方面的合作交流。此次赴瑞典展览作为协议实施的第一个成果，必将为双方在文物博物馆领域的深入持久合作打下坚实基础。

为了丰富河南群众精神文化生活，使文物保护成果惠及民生，我们特于3月至4月在洛阳博物馆先期进行预展。真诚期望通过这一展览，让河南民众感受青铜文化的独特魅力，体验中原文化的厚重精博，凝聚珍惜爱护历史文化遗产的共识，共同为打造华夏历史文明传承创新区贡献力量。

衷心祝愿展览圆满成功。

陈爱兰

河南省文物局 局长

Preface

    The Yellow River, winding in northern China, about 5464 km, the reaches area of about 795,000 square kms, is the sacred river in the heart of Chinese descendants, here is the earliest birthplace of civilization, also is the cradle of Chinese civilization. Henan, named for its mainly region in the south of the Yellow River. About ten thousand years ago, there entered the Neolithic Age, the ancestors lived by the river, enjoyed the river richly endowed, and sow the seeds of civilization. In the later Neolithic Age, the Yellow River reaches went into the vital period that early stage of established state. There are 2,000 years from the Xia Dynasty to the Warring States, royal families alternated, feudal marquises fought each other for power in the Central Plains, performed soul-stirring historical events, Henan had gradually become the center of Chinese civilization. A large number of exquisite cultural relics excavated in Henan reflects the living conditions of ancestors, highlighting the brilliant Chinese civilization.

    Xia, Shang and Zhou dynasties as long as two thousand years, is known as China's Bronze Age. During this period, Henan became the capitals of many royal families and feudal marquises. The capital of Xia Dynasty in Erlitou site in Yanshi, the capital of the Shang Dynasty in Zhengzhou, the Yin Ruins in Anyang and the capital of Eastern Zhou Dynasty in Luoyang, were all important centers of bronze casting at that time. A large number of bronze antiques unearthed in Henan, they have unique shape and exquisite craftsmanship, mainly represent the advanced level of metal smelting in the time. Because of its rare material and complex craftmanship , it is destined to its noble and mysterious merits, became the exclusive articles and ritual and grade symbol of the royal families and feudal marquises. The 117 selected items (set) in the exhibition, most are newly archaeological discoveries of Henan in recent years, basicly covering almost bronze objects category, comprehensively displaying the social outlook of this important historical period, reflecting the brilliant and colourful civilization of the bronze age of the Yellow River reaches.

The culture exchanges between Sweden and Henan, china have a long history. About 90 years ago, Mr.J.G. Andersson, Swedish scholar for the first time discovered and confirmed the neolithic cultural Site "yangshao culture" in Mianchi, Henan. Opened the door to cooperation and exchanges in the protection of cultural Heritage. In recent years, the extensive cooperation have been carried out between Henan institution of Cultural Heritage and the Sweden Museum, The Swedes have get understanding and familiar with the Central Plains culture increasingly. Especially in August, 2012, Henan Administration of Cultural Heritage and the Swedish national museum of world culture signed a cooperation agreement for five years, to further develop the cooperation and exchange in the protection of cultural relics, archaeological, scientific research, personnel training, and exhibition of antiques, etc. The exhibition to Sweden as the first results of the implementation of the Agreement, will lay a solid foundation for the deepening and sustainable cooperation in the fields of cultural relics and museum for both sides.

In order to enrich Henan people's spiritual and cultural life, make the heritage conservation achievement to benefit the people's livelihood, we are especially preview this exhibition at the Luoyang Museum in March to April, 2013. Sincerely hope that Henan people can feel the unique charm of the bronze culture, experience the deep connotation of the Central Plains culture from this exhibition, condense the consensus of cherishing historical and cultural heritage, and contribute our strength to build heritage and innovation of China historical civilization.

Sincerely wish the exhibition have a success.

Chen Ailan
Director of Henan Administration of Cultural Heritage

前 言

古之王者，择天下之中而立国。

位居中原腹地的河南，交通四面，辐辏八方，赋予了她发散包容的文化气质。远古时期，众多的氏族、部落在这里生聚发展。古国、方国在此创立，融合交流，兴衰存续。这里是中国文明起源的中心，是中国青铜文化萌芽、繁荣进而衰落全过程的缩影。

青铜器是中国文明的象征。夏商周时期的青铜器，既是生活用器，庙堂重器，又是权力和地位的物化符号。河南地区的青铜器见证了中国历史从邦国时期发展到王国时期，最终进入帝国时期的社会演进轨迹，见证了中国文明结束多元，陶熔一体，以中原为中心的历史格局形成的过程，见证了古代族群之间以中原为中心交往、会盟、征战、婚媾、商贸等的历史变革。

厚重悠久的历史，遗留下方国、王国、帝国的巍峨城池与赫赫宫阙，映象着往昔都邑的繁华；庄严的铜鼎与神秘纹饰，昭示着等级与王权的威严；斑驳的龟甲与浑朴的金文，记录着王室的祀典与征伐……这里发现了中国最早的青铜容器，最早的镶嵌青铜器；发现了中国最重达 875 公斤的商代后母戊方鼎，发现了中国最具代表性的方国青铜器群……

倘佯于这些饱蘸时间沧桑、散发着远古幽光的钟鼎彝器之间，从历史的深处，依稀回荡着中原文化天籁般美妙的音韵。

Preface

    Kings and emperors in ancient age, selected the center of the china to establish countries.

    Henan province located in the heart of central plains, the convenient transportation and specail region grant her the cultural character of exposure and embrace In ancient times, many tribes and clans lived in here, ancient states and town states established in here, they communicated for each other, waxed and waned. Here is the center and origin of Chinese civilization, the epitome of development history of Chinese bronze.

    Bronze is a symbol of Chinese civilization. During the Xia, Shang and Zhou dynasties, the bronze ware not only was the daily utensiles, the indispensable sacrificial vessels in the temple, but also was the representative of the power and status. Bronzes ware in the Henan province had witnessed the evolution track of the Chinese history that from nations to kingdoms and finally into the empires, the formation process that the historical pattern with the center of Central Plains of the Chinese civilization over diversification into integration, the historical facts that the communication, meetings of sovereigns or their deputies in ancient China to form alliances, wars, wedding, commerce and trade etc. among ancient ethnic groups with the center of Central Plains.

    Long glorious history, left lots of ruins of ancient town stats, states and empires, show the splendid of the former counties; stately bronze and mysterious decorations on bronzeware represented the majesty of the supreme kingship; mottled tortoise shell and unsophisticated inscriptions recorded grand royal sacrificial rites and campaigns and so on. Many famous bronze wares were discovered in here, such as the earliest bronze vessel, the earliest mosaic bronze in China; and the 875 kilograms HOUMuWu Square Ding of Shang dynasty which is the heaviest one in China, the town states bronze wares group which have the most representative in China and so on.

    Roam in these ancient precious amazing bronzes, across the history, we still can get the beautiful and unforgettable experience that the culture of Central Plains bring us.

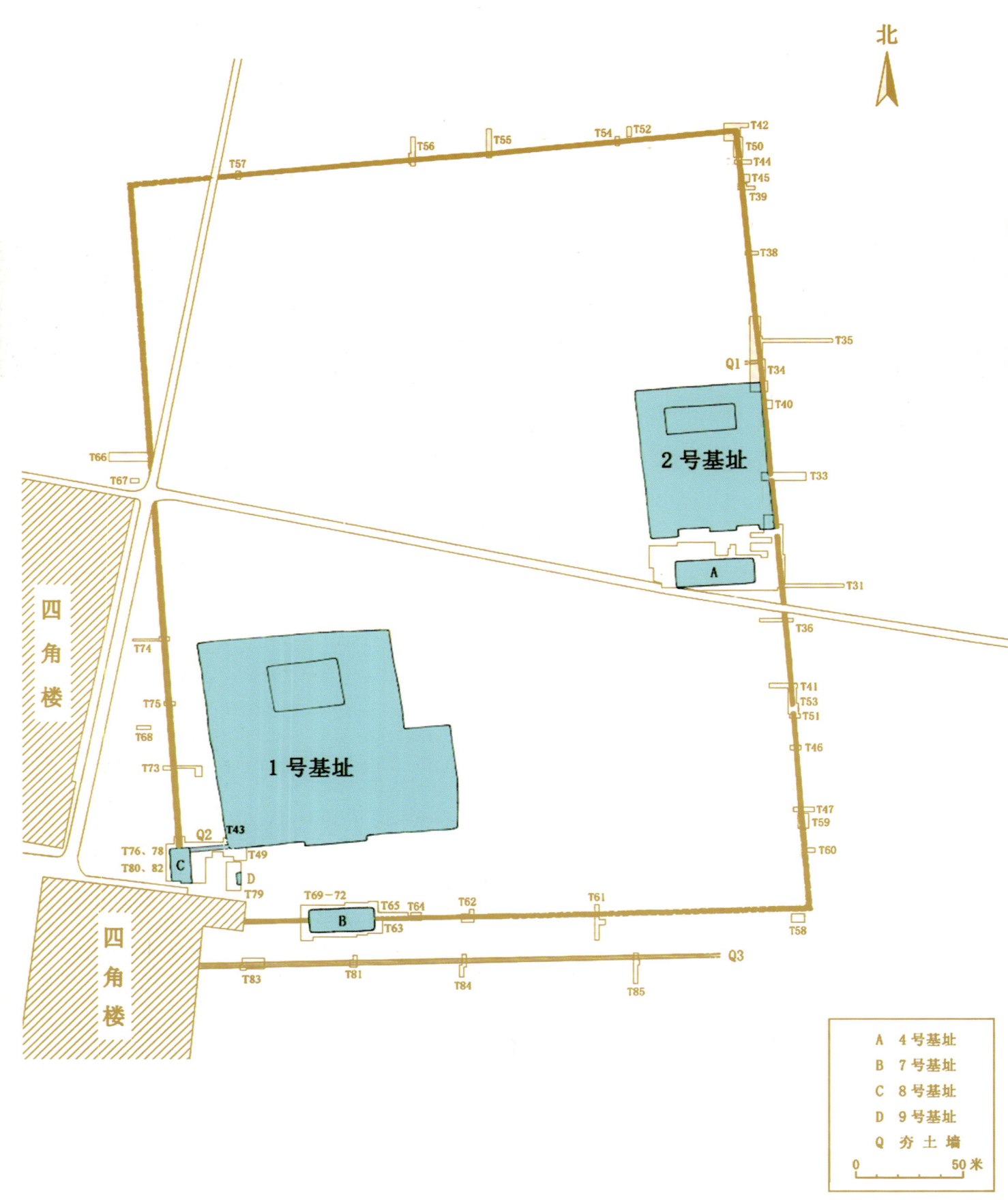

二里头遗址宫城平面图

王国崛起 器以藏礼 第一部分
夏代（公元前 2070 年～前 1600 年）

夏族是主要活动于豫西和晋南的古老部族。约公元前 21 世纪，相传大禹治水成功，被推选为夏族的首领，禹死后其子启继位，建立了中国历史上第一个王朝—夏。河南偃师二里头遗址的发掘，以及中原诸多夏代遗存的发现，证明了夏王朝在中原建都的事实，为揭开夏王朝神秘的面纱提供了重要实物依据。

Part I Xia Dynasty (2070B.C. ~1600B.C.)

Xia tribe was an ancient tribe mostly lived in the west of Henan province and the south of Shangxi province. About the 21st century BC, according to legend, as Dayu had the success in flood control , he was elected as the family leader, after his death, his son Qi succeed to the throne and established the first dynasty in Chinese history-Xia. The excavation of Erlitou ruins at Yanshi of Henan province, and many relics was found in Xia Dynasty in the Central Plains, proved the fact that Xia Dynasty found their capital in the Central Plains, and provided important basis in fact to know more about the mysterious of Xia dynasty .

偃师二里头青铜器

二里头遗址位于洛阳平原东部，距偃师市西南约九公里，总面积 3 平方公里，包括二里头、圪垱头、四角楼、案后村和辛庄五个自然村。遗址主要由中心区和一般居住活动区两部分组成，中心由宫殿区、贵族居住区、铸铜作坊、祭祀活动区组成。宫殿区南有绿松石制造作坊，一般居住活动区分布有小型墓葬及半地穴式居住遗址。该遗址发现了迄今所知我国最早的青铜铸造作坊和青铜礼器。

二里头遗址中心区有纵横交错的道路网，宫殿区围以方正规矩的城垣，宫城内分布着具有明确中轴线的大型建筑基址群，是一处经缜密规划、布局严整、且与后世中国古代都城营建一脉相承的大型都邑，其布局开中国古代都城规划制度之先河。

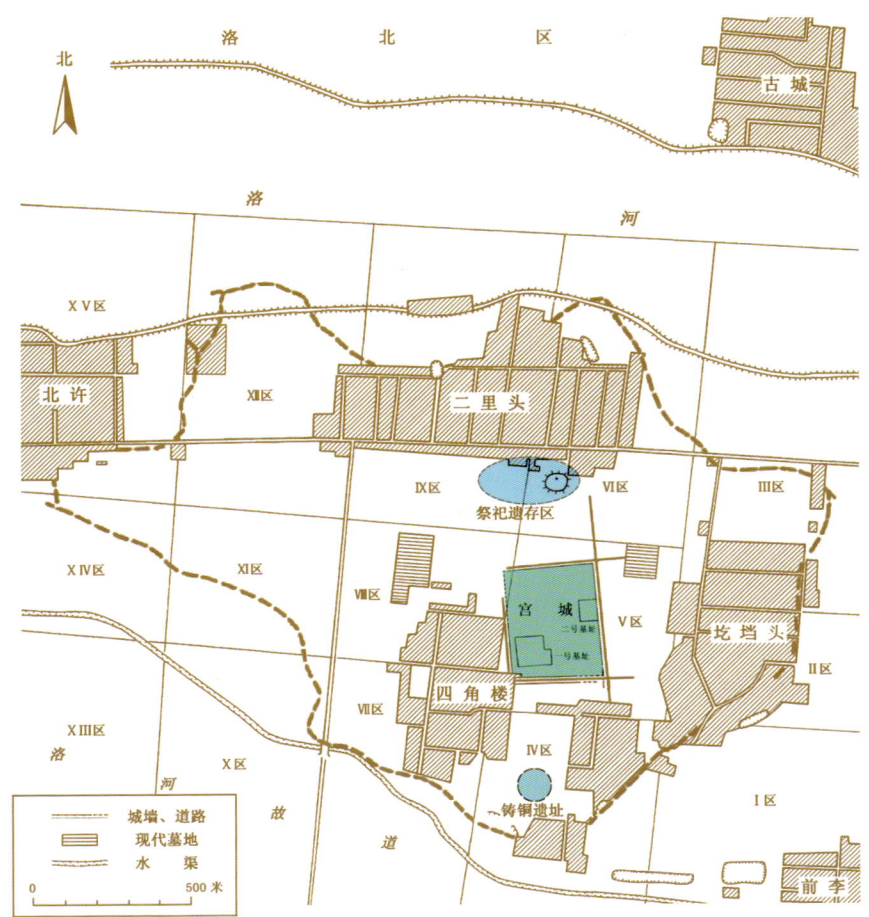

二里头遗址平面图

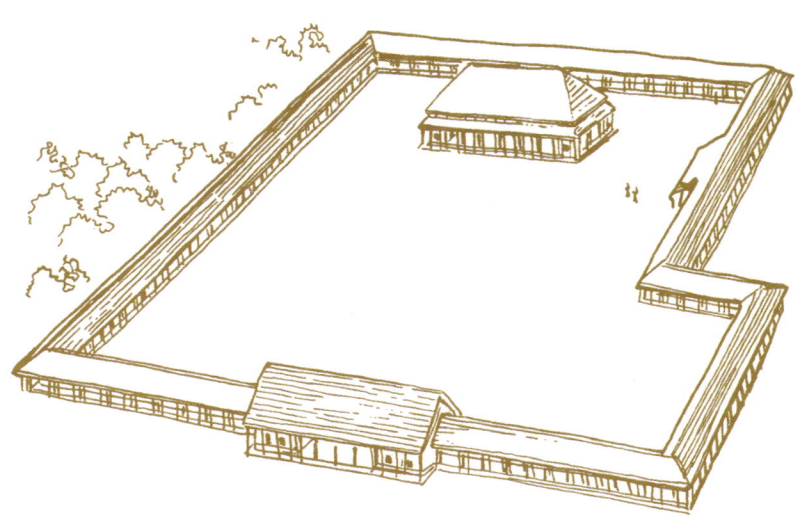

二里头遗址1号宫殿基址平面图和建筑复原图

方格纹鼎

夏代
1975年偃师二里头出土
高20厘米
洛阳博物馆藏
Bronze Ding with trellis pattern
Xia Dynasty
Excavated from Erlitou Site, Yanshi, 1975
Height: 20cm
Collected in Luoyang Museum

　　青铜鼎有烹煮肉食、实牲祭祀和宴飨等各种用途。相传夏禹收九牧之金铸九鼎，以象征九州。自此，鼎被视为立国重器，是国家和权力的象征。历商至周，都把定都或建立王朝称为"定鼎"。立国建都以定鼎，而国灭族亡则鼎迁。

乳钉纹爵

夏代
1975年偃师二里头出土
高 22.5 厘米
洛阳博物馆藏
Bronze Jue with nipple studs pattern
Xia Dynasty
Excavated from Erlitou Site, Yanshi, 1975
Height: 22.5cm
Collected in Luoyang Museum

  中国最早的青铜饮酒器，距今 3500 年左右。
  考古工作者曾在偃师二里头遗址中发掘出炼渣、炼铜坩埚和陶范残片，证明二里头文化已经有了冶炼和制作青铜器的作坊。从目前二里头发现的夏代青铜器看，一开始就具备了礼器、乐器、兵器三大类别，可见中国青铜时代"器以藏礼"的特性。

素面爵

夏代
1973年偃师二里头出土
高11.4厘米
洛阳博物馆藏
Bronze Jue
Xia Dynasty
Excavated from Erlitou Site, Yanshi, 1973
Height: 11.4cm
Collected in Luoyang Museum

神秘王朝 雄奇瑰宝 第二部分
商代（公元前 1600 年～前 1046 年）

商族是活动在黄河下游的古老部族。夏朝末年，商的势力由黄河下游发展到黄河中游，渗入夏人统治地区。约公元前 1600 年，商汤灭夏建立商朝，至前 11 世纪殷纣灭亡，凡 17 世 30 王 500 余年，特别是盘庚迁殷至纣之灭 273 年间，中原一直是殷王朝统治中心。70 年来的考古发掘表明，商人不仅将青铜文明推向鼎盛，甲骨文的出现也使得中华文明从此史书有载。

Part II Shang Dynasty (1600B.C. ~1046B.C.)

Shang tribe was an ancient tribe mostly lived in the lower reaches of the Yellow River. In the end of Xia dynasty, the influence of Shang tribe developed from the lower reaches to the middle reaches of the Yellow River, and had permeate into the region by Xia tribe ruled. About the 1600 BC, between the Xia Dynasty was succeeded by the Shangtang and Shang Dynasty was overthrew in 11th century, there had about 500 years, sepcially in the 273 years which from the King Panggeng firstly moved the capital to Yin until Shang Dynasty was overthrew, the Central Plains always was the centre of ruling of Shang Dynasty. The 70 years of archaeological excavations indicated that Shang people pushed the bronze civilization to it culminates and the emergence of carapace-bone-script made the Chinese civilization can be written down.

郑州商城青铜器

郑州商城遗址是商代前期的都城遗址，总面积约25平方公里。城址平面近似长方形，分内城和外城两部分。外城是中小贵族和平民居住及墓葬区，也有奴隶的劳作场所，分布铸铜、制陶、制骨等作坊遗址。内城四周高筑约7公里的城墙，内有多座大型宫殿遗址，是商王室和贵族的生活居住区。这里窖藏、墓葬出土了大批青铜器，是中国商代早期青铜器的代表。

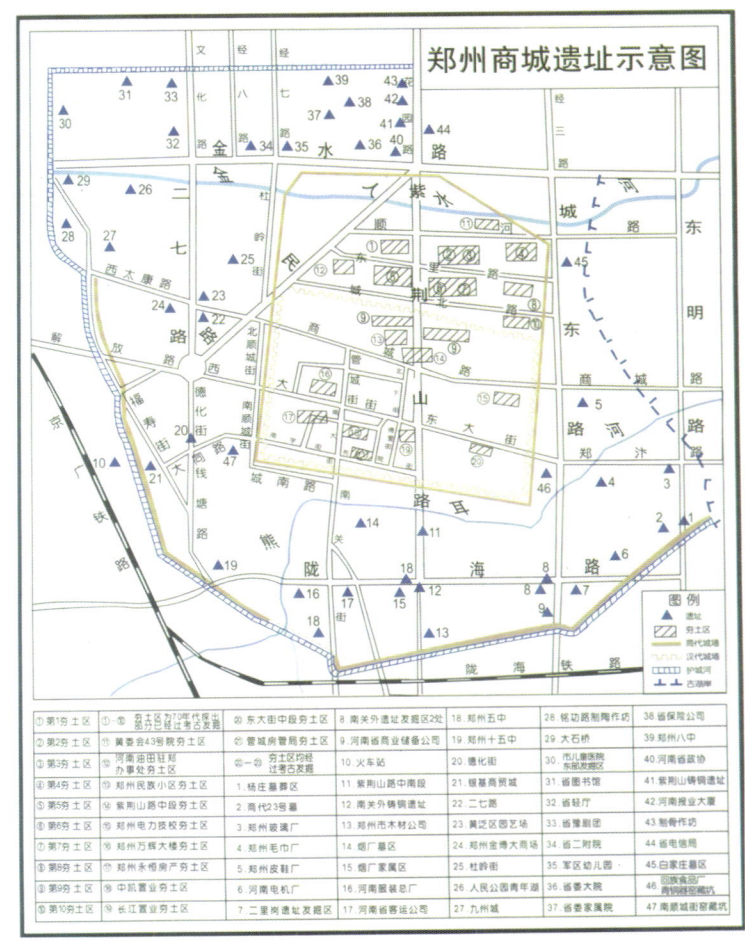

1982年向阳回族食品厂窖藏坑发掘现场

兽面乳钉纹方鼎

商代前期
1982年郑州向阳回族食品厂窖藏坑出土
高81厘米
郑州博物馆藏
Squared bronze Ding with beast-mask and nipple studs patterns
Early period of Shang Dynasty
Excavated from the Hoard of Xiangyang food factory of Hui nationality at Zhengzhou, 1982
Height: 81cm
Collected in Zhengzhou Museum

此鼎深腹、四足，沉稳庄重。这是中国最早的大型青铜方鼎之一。其采用多范分铸而成，说明商代早期已具备了相当高的冶铸水平。

兽面纹大口尊

商代前期
1982年郑州向阳回族食品厂窖藏坑出土
高37厘米
郑州博物馆藏
Bronze Zun with beast-mask pattern
Early period of Shang Dynasty
Excavated from the Hoard of Xiangyang food factory of Hui nationality at Zhengzhou,1982
Height:37cm
Collected in Zhengzhou Museum

兽面纹鼎

商代前期
1982年郑州北二七路商墓出土
高23.7厘米
河南省文物考古研究所藏
Bronze Ding with beast-mask pattern
Early period of Shang Dynasty
Excavated from the tomb of Shang Dynasty at Erqi road, north of Zhengzhou, 1982
Height: 23.7cm
Collected in Henan Archeology and Cultural Relics Research Institute

兽面纹斝

商代前期
1982年郑州北二七路商墓出土
高33厘米
河南省文物考古研究所藏
Bronze Jia with beast-mask pattern
Early period of Shang Dynasty
Excavated from the tomb of Shang Dynasty at Erqi road, north of Zhengzhou, 1982
Height:33cm
Collected in Henan Archeology and Cultural Relics Research Institute

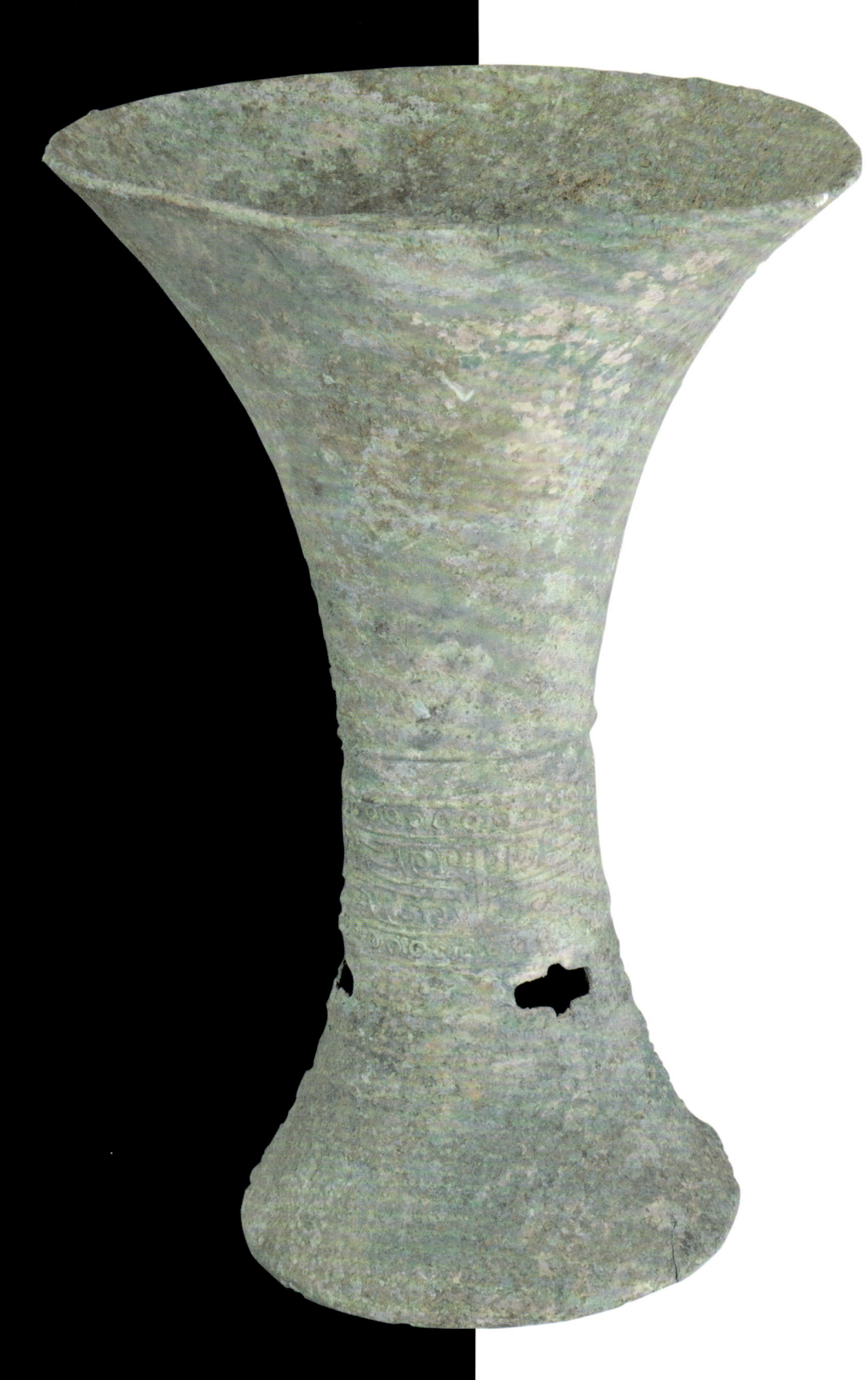

云纹觚

商代前期
1982年郑州向阳回族食品厂窖藏出土
高24厘米
河南省文物考古研究所藏
Bronze Gu with cloud pattern
Early period of Shang Dynasty
Excavated from the Hoard of Xiangyang food factory of Hui nationality at Zhengzhou, 1982
Height: 24cm
Collected in Henan Archeology and Cultural Relics Research Institute

兽面纹爵

商代前期
1982年郑州北二七路商墓出土
高 19.7 厘米
河南省文物考古研究所藏
Bronze Jue with beast-mask pattern
Early period of Shang Dynasty
Excavated from the tomb of Shang Dynasty at
Erqi road, north of Zhengzhou, 1982
Height: 19.7cm
Collected in Henan Archeology and Cultural
Relics Research Institute

安阳殷墟青铜器

公元前1300年前后，盘庚迁都于殷（今安阳市小屯一带），至纣王亡国，整个商代后期以此为都。清末殷墟甲骨文的发现，使商代的历史被确立为信史；经过80多年、几代考古学者的不懈努力，在安阳洹河两岸约24平方公里的范围内发现并发掘了宫殿宗庙区、王陵区、祭祀场所、墓葬区、手工业作坊和居民区，出土了数以万计的铜、陶、玉、石、骨、蚌等遗物和十数万片甲骨，掩埋了三千多年的商代最后都城的秘密逐步被揭开。

殷墟出土品类众多的青铜器，造型诡谲神秘，纹饰威严凝重，蕴含着深厚粗犷的原始张力和艺术魅力，反映了殷商先民特有的宗教情感和审美观念。这时人们已掌握着更为先进的铸造工艺，铸造出令人叹为观止的国之重器是中国青铜器铸造的第一个高峰期。

"妇好"墓发掘现场

"妇好"墓圹复原

036 神秘王朝 雄奇瑰宝

"妇好"方尊

商代后期
1976年安阳殷墟出土
高43厘米
河南博物院藏

Square bronze Zun inscribed "fu hao"
Late period of Shang Dynasty
Excavated from Yin Ruins, Anyang, 1976
Height: 43cm
Collected in Henan Museum

兽面纹方斝

商代后期
1976 年安阳殷墟出土
高 21 厘米
河南博物院藏

Square bronze Jia with beast-mask pattern
Late period of Shang Dynasty
Excavated from Yin Ruins, Anyang, 1976
Height: 21cm
Collected in Henan Museum

"妇好"方斝

商代后期
1976年安阳殷墟出土
高 67.6 厘米
河南博物院藏
Square bronze Jia inscribed "fu hao"
Late period of Shang Dynasty
Excavated from Yin Ruins, Anyang, 1976
Height: 67.6cm
Collected in Henan Museum

"妇好"鸮尊

商代后期
1976年安阳殷墟出土
高45.9厘米
河南博物院藏
Bronze Zun with owl-shaped inscribed "fu hao"
Late period of Shang Dynasty

"司母辛"觥

商代后期
1976年安阳殷墟出土
高 36 厘米
河南博物院藏
Bronze Gong inscribed "Si Mu Xin"
Late period of Shang Dynasty
Excavated from Yin Ruins, Anyang, 1976
Height: 36cm
Collected in Henan Museum

　　觥是盛酒器，出现于商代晚期，沿用至西周早期。这件觥作鸟兽合体形，器物前部为立兽状，后部为鸟形。兽头上双角自然曲蜷，中脊至尾为卷龙形，兽首状弓形鋬。通体满花。盖内与器身内均有"司母辛"三字铭文。该觥造型雄奇，立兽似牛非牛的艺术性夸张，增添了器物的瑰伟奇丽之美。纹饰细腻精致，器身布满盘绕回旋的龙蛇纹、鸟纹，具有较强的时代特征。铭文"司母辛"中的"母辛"与"妇好"实为一人。妇好是生称，辛是庙号，司是祭祀。此器是商王武丁子辈对其母妇好所做的祭器。

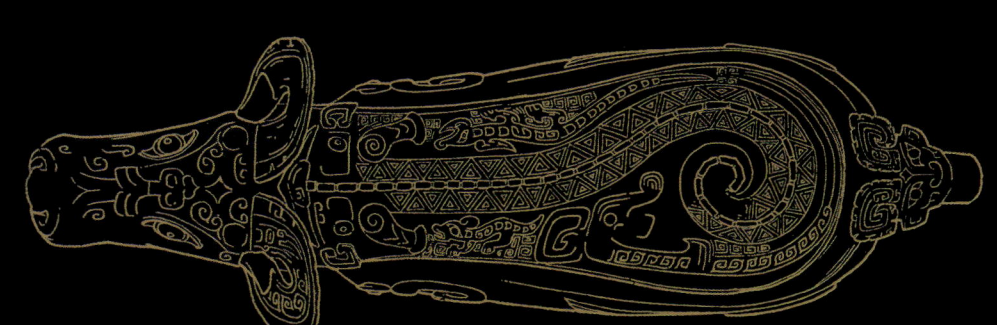

弦纹甗

商代后期
1976年安阳殷墟出土
高48.4厘米
安阳博物馆藏
Bronze Yan with bow string pattern
Late period of Shang Dynasty
Excavated from Yin Ruins, Anyang, 1976
Height: 48.4cm
Collected in Anyang Museum

火纹方罍

商代后期
1976年安阳殷墟出土
高41.2厘米
安阳博物馆藏

Square bronze Lei with spark pattern
Late period of Shang Dynasty
Excavated from Yin Ruins, Anyang, 1976
Height: 41.2cm
Collected in Anyang Museum

曲内戈

商代后期
1976年安阳殷墟出土
长27.5厘米
安阳博物馆藏
Bronze curved-tang Ge
Late period of Shang Dynasty
Excavated from Yin Ruins, Anyang, 1976
Length: 27.5cm
Collected in Anyang Museum

蕉叶纹矛

商代后期
1976年安阳殷墟出土
长25.5厘米
安阳博物馆藏
Bronze Mao with banana leaf pattern
Late period of Shang Dynasty
Excavated from Yin Ruins, Anyang, 1976
Length: 25.5 cm
Collected in Anyang Museum

商代车马器示意图
The schematic diagram of horses and chariots device in the Shang Dynasty

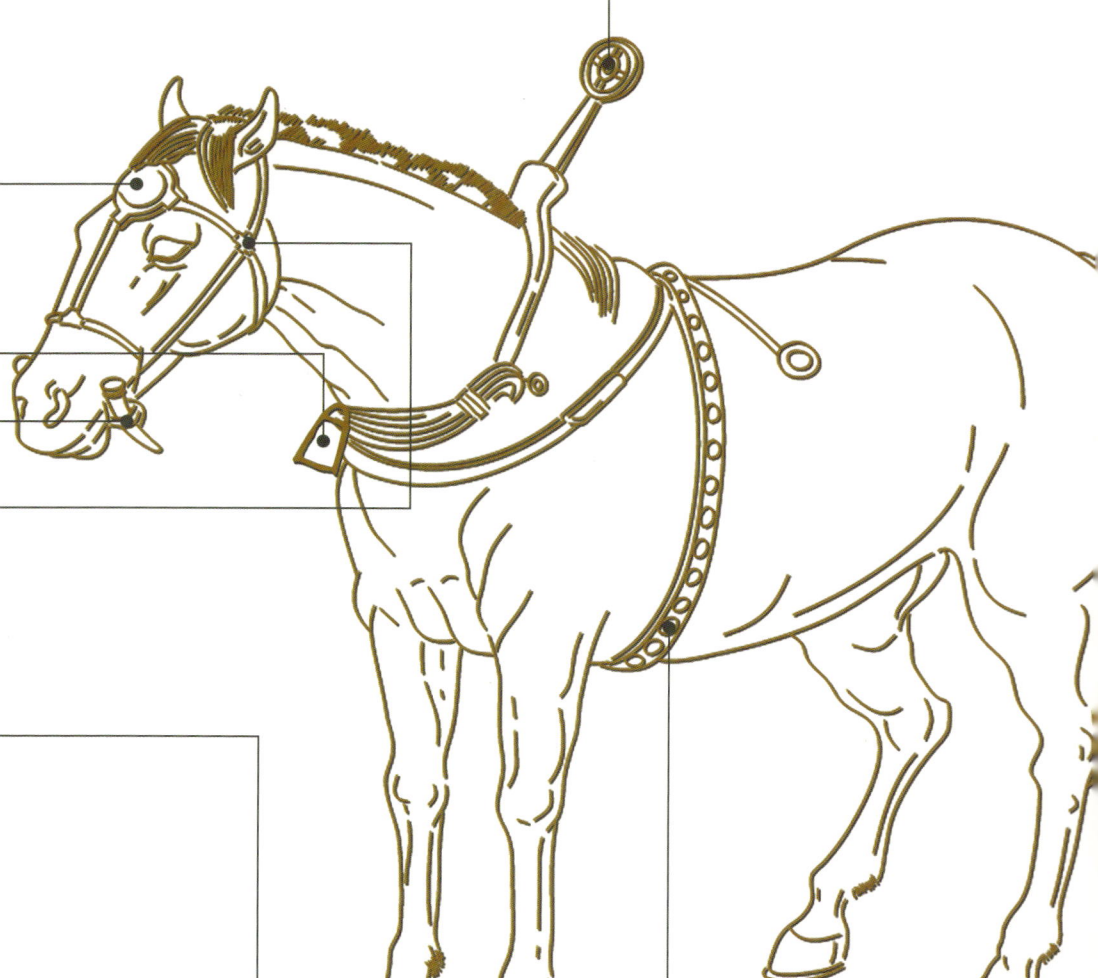

蝉纹銮铃

长 14.6 厘米
Length:14.6cm

旋涡纹泡

直径 2.8 厘米
Diameter:2.8cm

嵌绿松石泡

直径 3.4 厘米
Diameter:3.4cm

兽面纹泡

直径 4.3 厘米
Diameter:4.3cm

兽面纹当卢

高 5.44 厘米
Height:5.44cm

素面铃

长 5.45 厘米
Length:5.45 cm

素面马镳

长 7.5 厘米
Length:7.5cm

兽面纹铃

高 9.15 厘米
Height:9.15cm

素面十字节约

长 4.05 厘米
Length:4.05cm

十字节约

长 5.1 厘米
Length:5.1cm

商代车马器　安阳殷墟商代晚期车马坑

商代车马器

商代后期
1976 年安阳殷墟出土
安阳博物馆藏
Bronze ornament of bridle with animal-mask pattern (Dang Lu)
Late period of Shang Dynasty
Excavated from Yin Ruins, Anyang, 1976
Collected in Anyang Museum

商代晚期，马车的使用已经十分普遍了。据史书记载，商人的先祖相土时，就能用四匹马来驾车了。到了商代晚期的武丁时期，商朝国力强大，到处征伐，使用大规模的战车，开拓疆土。殷墟发现的大量车马坑以及车马器就是当时马车普遍使用的写照。

兽头形泡

长 2.7 厘米
Length:2.7cm

兽头形泡

长 2.65 厘米
Length:2.65cm

蕉叶纹车軎

长 17 厘米
Length:17cm

云雷纹车饰

长 14.8 厘米
Length:14.8cm

面泡

3.7 厘米
eter:3.7cm

素面车饰

长 12.2 厘米
Length:12.2cm

蕉叶纹车軎、辖

长 17.8 厘米
Length:17.8cm

素面
直径
Diam

圆涡纹泡
直径 3.3 厘米
Diameter:3.3cm

圆涡纹泡
直径 3.3 厘米
Diameter:3.3cm

罗山莽张息国铜器

在商王朝疆域的边沿处，分布着许多商王朝未直接进行统治的小国，被称作"方"或"邦"。"息"国是商王朝偏南的方国之一，是中原文化与南方交汇的重要地区。

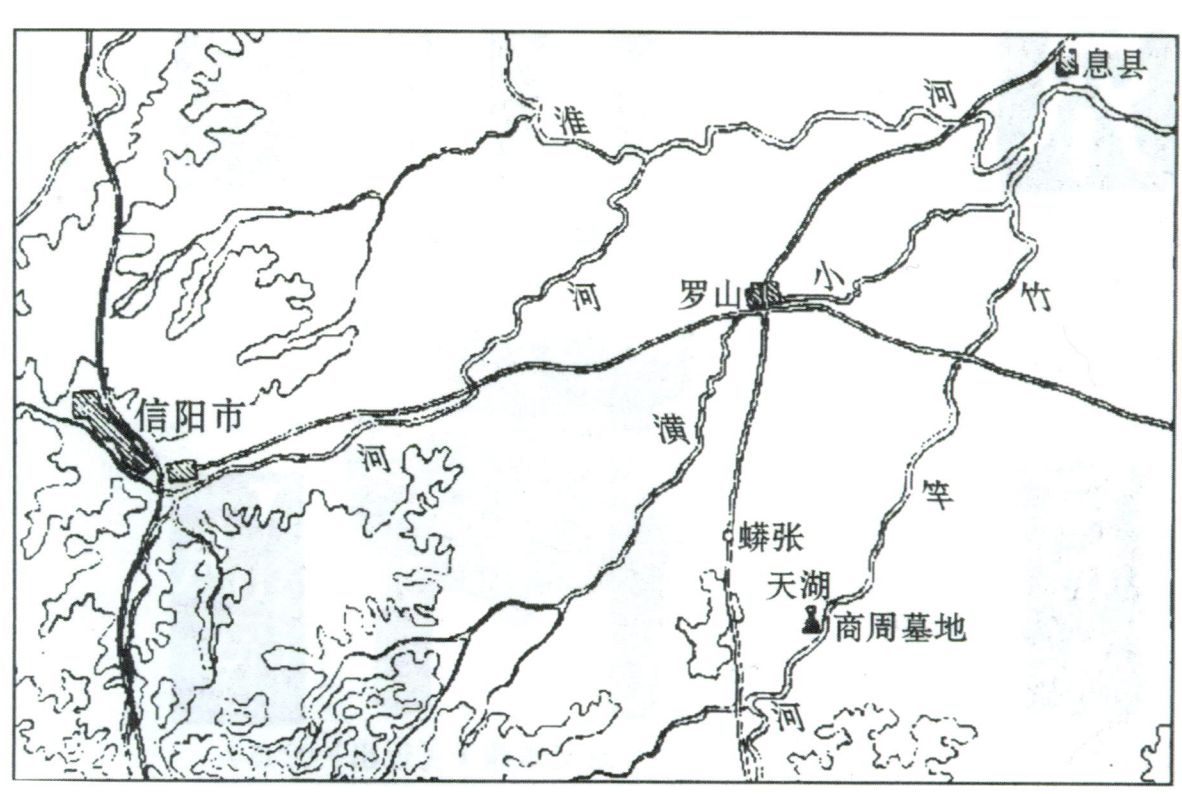

罗山天湖、蟒张墓葬地理位置图

兽面纹斝

商代后期
1991年信阳罗山莽张出土
高34厘米
河南省文物考古研究所藏
Bronze Jia with beast-mask pattern
Late period of Shang Dynasty
Excavated from Mangzhang, Luoshan, Xinyang, 1991
Height: 34cm
Collected in Henan Archeology and Cultural Relics Research Institute

兽面纹觚

商代后期
1991年信阳罗山莽张出土
高30.5厘米
河南省文物考古研究所藏
Bronze Gu with beast-mask pattern
Late period of Shang Dynasty
Excavated from Mangzhang,Luoshan,Xinyang,1991
Height:30.5cm
Collected in Henan Archeology and Cultural Relics Research Institute

兽面纹簋

商代后期
1991年信阳罗山莽张出土
高16.7厘米
河南省文物考古研究所藏
Bronze Gui with beast-mask pattern
Late period of Shang Dynasty
Excavated from Mangzhang, Luoshan, Xinyang, 1991
Height:16.7cm
Collected in Henan Archeology and Cultural Relics Research Institute

"息父辛"爵

商代后期
1980年信阳罗山莽张出土
高19.7厘米
信阳博物馆藏
Bronze Jue inscribed "Xi Fu Xin"
Late period of Shang Dynasty
Excavated from Mangzhang, Luoshan, Xinyang, 1980
Height: 19.7cm
Collected in Xinyang museum

国王与诸侯—中国河南青铜文明 059

060 神秘王朝 雄奇瑰宝

兽面纹鼎

商代后期
1980年信阳罗山莽张出土
高 25.6 厘米
信阳博物馆藏
Bronze Jue with beast-mask pattern
Late period of Shang Dynasty
Excavated from Mangzhang, Luoshan, Xinyang, 1980
Height: 25.6cm
Collected in Xinyang museum

礼乐大成 赫赫成周　第三部分
西周时期（公元前1046年~前771年）

周族是活动在中国西部泾、渭流域的古老部族。公元前1046年，周武王灭商，建立周朝。西周王朝建立初，是以镐京（西安长安区）为国都，为加强对中原地区广大殷遗民及东南地区方国的统治，迁都中土"成周"洛阳。成为统治中国的又一政治、经济、文化的中心。

周朝初年采用分封政策，"封建亲戚，以藩屏周"，周王室把同姓宗亲和有功的或有势力的异姓贵族分封到各地，建立诸侯国，以巩固其新的政权。中原地处天下之中、殷商旧地，先后有70多个诸侯在此受封。河南境内卫国、虢国、应国等西周诸侯国贵族墓地的相继发现，进一步揭示了西周宗法制度的真实面貌。周武王师渡盟津，决战牧野，伐纣灭商。

Part III Western Zhou Dynasty (1046B.C.~771B.C.)

Zhou tribal was an ancient tribal mostly lived in the Jing and Wei River basin in the west of China. In 1046 BC, King Wu overthrew Shang Dynasty, and established the Zhou Dynasty. Western Zhou Dynasty was established early in Gao (Chang'an District, Xi'an City) as its capital, in order to strengthened its rule over the majority of the descendants of the Shang Dynasty and ancient states which in southeast of China, moved the capital to Luoyang City which in the middle of China. Become another centre which was political, economic and cultural of ruling of China.

There was the policy of feudal system of enfeoffment in the early of Zhou Dynasty. The Zhou royal confered titles and territories to their kinsmen and the different surname nobility who had active forces to the country, built vassal state to consolidate its new regime. The Central Plains at the center of China, there had been over 70 princes were confered. The aristocratic cemeteries such as Wei state, Guo State, Ying state of the Western Zhou Dynasty vassal states in Henan province have been found, extensive research have revealed the real Western Zhou Dynasty patriarchal system. King Wu of Zhou Dynasty marched through the Mengjin, decisive battle at Muye, overthrew the Shang Dynasty.

洛阳西周王室青铜器

周公营建洛邑后，依据周制，参酌殷礼，建立一套比较完整的宗法等级、世袭制度。西周中期，逐步形成一系列等级森严的典章制度和礼仪规定，体现在贵族祭神享祖、礼仪交往、宴飨宾客所使用礼器数量与规格上，即所谓"藏礼于器"。洛阳出土的大批西周王室贵族青铜器如著名的保尊、保卣、作册大方鼎、令方彝、矢令簋、叔牝方彝、召伯虎盨、王妊簋、太保戈、康伯壶、丰伯剑等，均为这一时期具有代表性的铜器。不仅如此，在北窑等地还发现了大规模的铸铜遗址，表明洛阳是西周青铜铸造业的中心之一。

叔牝方彝局部纹饰

"叔牝" 方彝

西周
洛阳小李村出土
高 32.6 厘米
洛阳博物馆藏
Square bronze Yi inscribed "Shu pin"
Western Zhou Dynasty
Excavated from XiaoLi Village, Luoyang City
Height: 32.6cm
Collected in Luoyang Museum

  方彝是一种典型的西周早期盛酒器。盖做成古建筑的屋顶型，极似商周王室宫殿建筑的大屋顶。通体饰云雷纹为地，高扉棱为鼻梁的凸目兽面纹。唯口沿下、圈足及盖顶上是一周凤鸟纹。纹样繁密工细，铸做精工。更为可贵的是，盖及腹内铸铭文3行12字"叔牝赐贝于王姒用作宝尊彝"，大意是叔牝得到了周王之妃"王姒"的赏赐而做铜器。

兽面纹簋

西周
洛阳出土
高 14.2 厘米　口径 18.6 厘米
洛阳博物馆藏
Bronze Gui with beast-mask motif
Western Zhou Dynasty
Excavated from Luoyang City
Height:14.2cm　Mouth:18.6cm
Collected in Luoyang Museum

070 礼乐大成 赫赫成周

双面人四管器座

西周
洛阳林校出土
高 15.5 厘米
洛阳博物馆藏

Pedestals in the shape of double-faced person
Western Zhou Dynasty
Excavated from Forestry School in Luoyang City
Height:15.5cm
Collected in Luoyang Museum

"白懋父"簋

西周
洛阳北窑出土
高14.5厘米　口径18.9厘米
洛阳博物馆藏
Bronze Gui inscribed "Bai Mao Fu"
Western Zhou Dynasty
Excavated from Beiyao, Luoyang City
Height: 14.5cm Mouth: 18.9cm
Collected in Luoyang Museum

074 礼乐大成 赫赫成周

四足方盉

西周
洛阳北窑出土
高19厘米　口径12.5厘米
洛阳博物馆藏
Bronze He with four feet
Western Zhou Dynasty
Excavated from Beiyao, Luoyang City
Height: 19cm　Mouth: 12.5cm
Collected in Luoyang Museum

云雷纹鼎

西周
洛阳出土
高 43 厘米 口径 32.6 厘米
洛阳博物馆藏
Bronze Ding with cloud and thunder motif
Western Zhou Dynasty
Excavated from Luoyang City
Height:43cm Mouth:32.6cm
Collected in Luoyang Museum

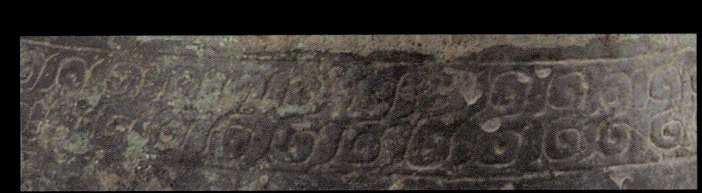

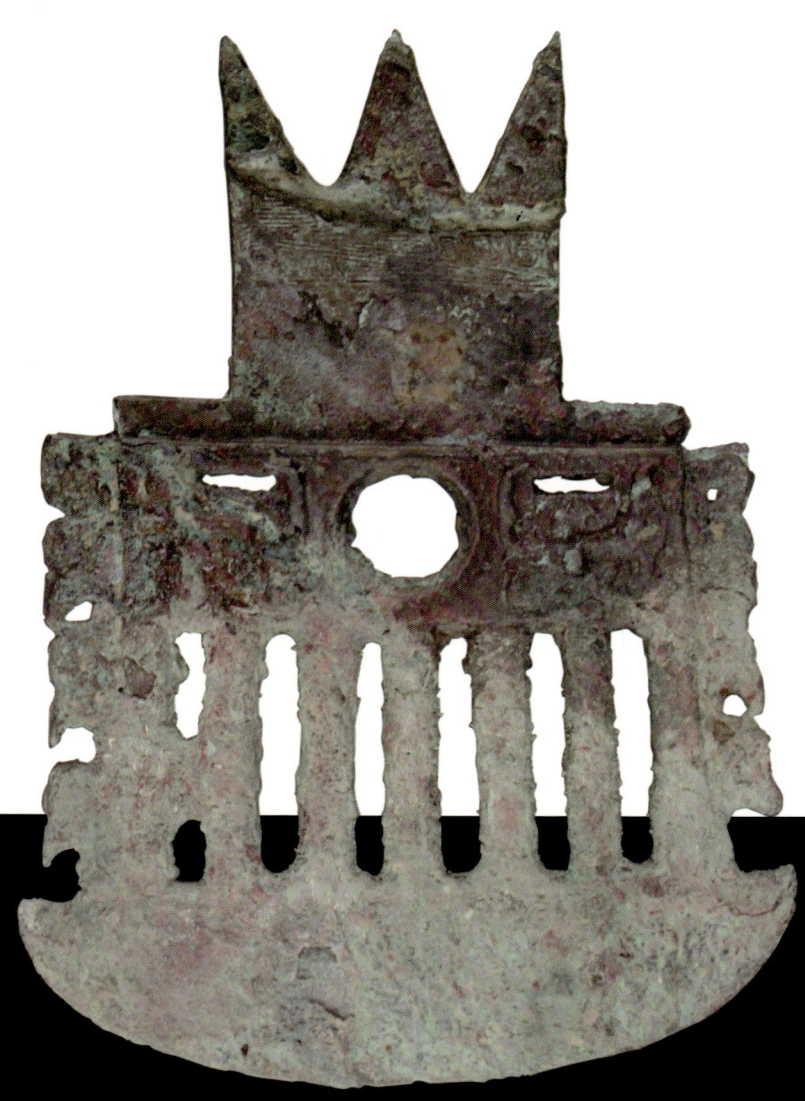

兽面纹钺

西周
洛阳林校出土
长 18.2 厘米 宽 12 厘米
洛阳博物馆藏
Bronze Yue with beast-mask motif
Western Zhou Dynasty
Excavated from Forestry School in Luoyang City
Length:18.2cm Width:12cm
Collected in Luoyang Museum

铜矛

西周
洛阳机瓦厂出土
长 15.5 厘米
洛阳博物馆藏
Bronze Mao, a spear
Western Zhou Dynasty
Excavated from Luoyang City
Length:15.5cm
Collected in Luoyang Museum

虎纹卷首刀

西周
洛阳林校出土
长 29 厘米
洛阳博物馆藏

Bronze undulated-tip knife with tiger motif
Western Zhou Dynasty
Excavated from Forestry School of Luoyang City
Length: 29cm
Collected in Luoyang Museum

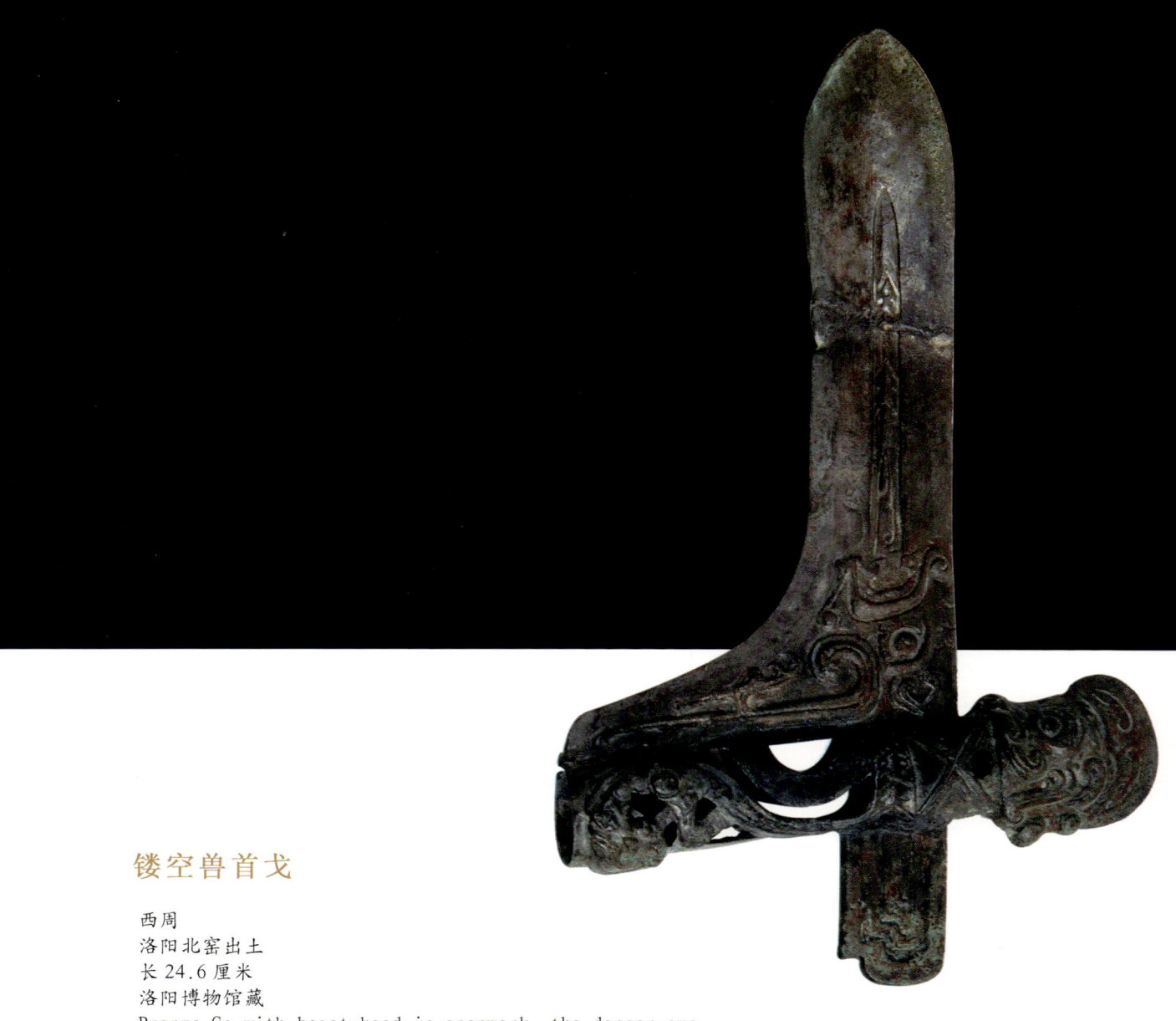

镂空兽首戈

西周
洛阳北窑出土
长 24.6 厘米
洛阳博物馆藏
Bronze Ge with beast-head in openwork, the dagger-axe
Western Zhou Dynasty
Excavated from Beiyao, Luoyang City
Length: 24.6cm
Collected in Luoyang Museum

凤鸟纹马镳及马衔

西周
洛阳机瓦厂出土
镳长 20 厘米　衔长 9.5 厘米
洛阳博物馆藏
Bronze curb chain and bit of chariot with phoenix motif
Western Zhou Dynasty
Excavated from Luoyang City
Length of Chain:15.7cm　Length of Bit:9.5cm
Collected in Luoyang Museum

"兽"当卢

西周
洛阳机瓦厂出土
长20.2厘米
洛阳博物馆藏

Bronze ornament of bidle inscribed "Shou"
Western Zhou Dynasty
Excavated from Luoyang City
Length:20.2cm
Collected in Luoyang Museum

"南"干首

西周
洛阳机瓦厂出土
长 27.34 厘米
洛阳博物馆藏
Bronze Ganshou inscribed "Nan", weapon
Western Zhou Dynasty
Excavated from Luoyang City
Length:27.34cm
Collected in Luoyang Museum

镂空銮铃

西周
洛阳机瓦厂出土
长 15.7 厘米
洛阳博物馆藏
Bronze bell in openwork
Western Zhou Dynasty
Excavated from Luoyang City
Length:15.7cm
Collected in Luoyang Museum

夔龙牛首纹车饰

西周
洛阳北窑出土
高 18.6 厘米
洛阳博物馆藏
Bronze chariot ornament with dragon of ox-head shape
Western Zhou Dynasty
Excavated from Beiyao, Luoyang City
Height: 18.6cm
Collected in Luoyang Museum

镂空兽头车饰

西周
洛阳北窑出土
高 11.2 厘米
洛阳博物馆藏
Bronze chariot ornament of beast-head in openwork
Western Zhou Dynasty
Excavated from Beiyao, Luoyang City
Height: 11.2cm
Collected in Luoyang Museum

鹿邑太清宫殷遗民青铜器

　　鹿邑太清宫位于河南省鹿邑县。1997 年河南省文物考古研究在此发掘商末周初一座双墓道中字形大墓，出土大批组合完整的商遗民青铜器，是商周考古的一次重大发现。该墓全长 47.75 米、宽 7 米。出土各类器物 1000 余件，殉人 13 具。墓主"长子口"为商末贵族，周初归顺被册封为长国之君。其丰富多彩的、极富商文化特色的大批青铜器的随葬展现了一代方国君王的气派。

鹿邑太清宫"长子口"墓发掘现场

兽面纹鼎

西周
鹿邑长子口墓出土
高50.8厘米　口径38厘米
河南省文物考古研究所藏
Bronze Ding with beast-mask motif
Western Zhou Dynasty
Excavated from the tomb of Zhangzikou in Luyi County
Height:50.8cm Mouth:38cm
Collected in Henan Archeology and Cultural Relics Research Institute

国王与诸侯—中国河南青铜文明 093

094 礼乐大成 赫赫成周

"长子口"鼎

西周
鹿邑长子口墓出土
高23.2厘米 口径17.6厘米
河南省文物考古研究所藏
Bronze Ding inscribed "Zhangzikou"
Western Zhou Dynasty
Excavated from the tomb of Zhangzikou in Luyi County
Height:23.2cm Mouth:17.6cm
Collected in Henan Archeology and Cultural Relics Research Institute

"析子孙"方鼎

西周
鹿邑长子口墓出土
高 21.6 厘米
河南省文物考古研究所藏
Bronze Ding inscribed "Xizisun"
Western Zhou Dynasty
Excavated from the tomb of Zhangzikou in Luyi County
Height: 21.6cm
Collected in Henan Archeology and Cultural Relics Research Institute

"长子口"方罍

西周
鹿邑长子口墓出土
高47.6厘米
河南省文物考古研究所藏
Square bronze Lei inscribed "Zhangzikou"
Western Zhou Dynasty
Excavated from the tomb of Zhangzikou in Luyi County
Height:47.6cm
Collected in Henan Archeology and Cultural Relics Research Institute

  盖呈四阿攒顶式，中间置方形钮柱，钮顶亦为四阿屋顶式。器口呈长方形，宽平沿，直颈，溜肩，深腹，平底，长方形圈足外撇。肩部两侧置对应的半环形兽首耳，衔大圆环，两耳之间的腹下部一侧置半环形兽鼻钮。盖、器身四角及四面中部均有扉棱。器表饰以云雷纹为地的夔龙纹和兽面纹。器口内壁有铭文"长子口"三字。

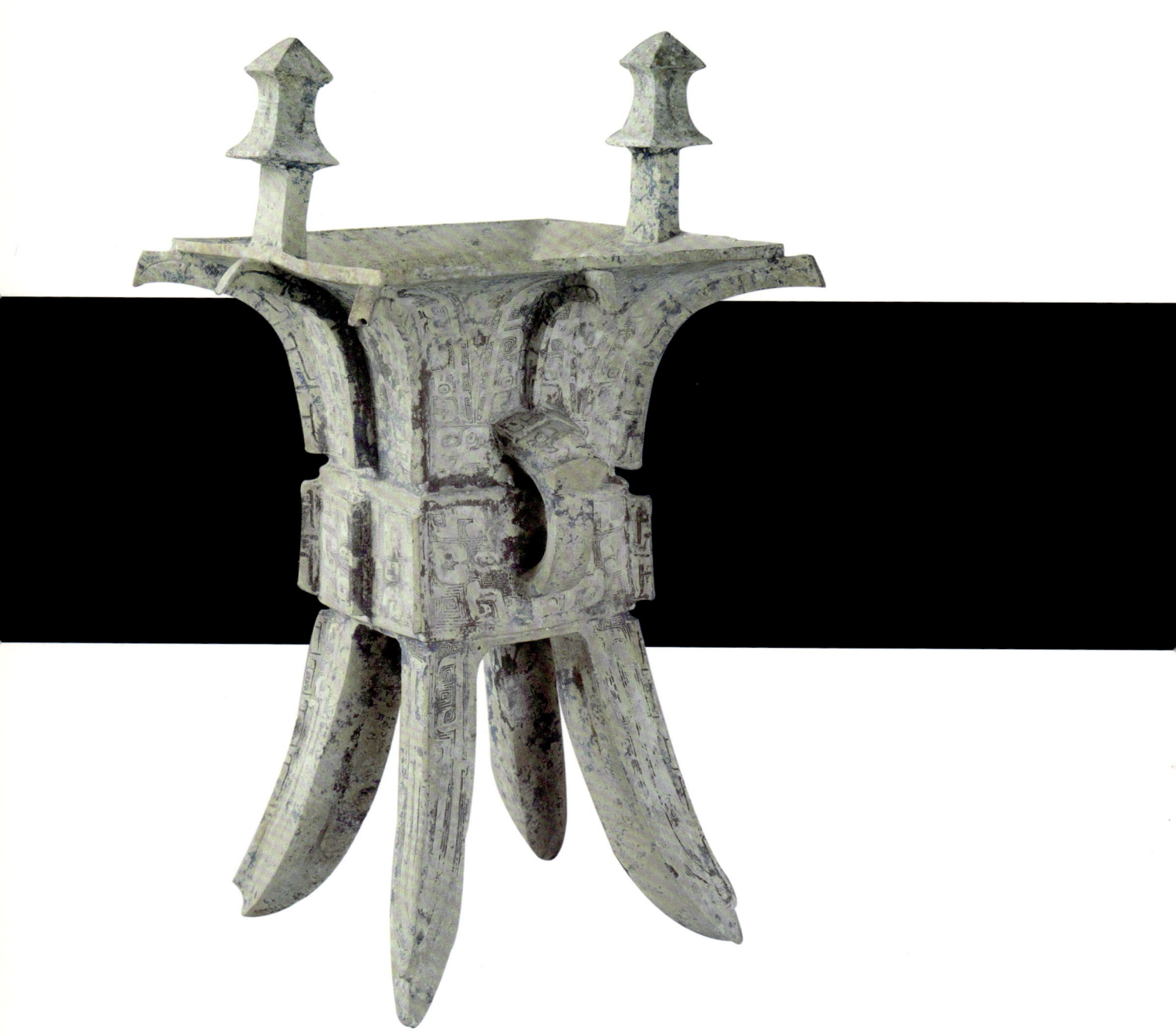

100 礼乐大成 赫赫成周

"长子口"方斝

西周
鹿邑长子口墓出土
高 39 厘米
河南省文物考古研究所藏
Square bronze Jia inscribed "Zhangzikou"
Western Zhou Dynasty
Excavated from the tomb of Zhangzikou in Luyi County
Height:39cm
Collected in Henan Archeology and Cultural Relics Research Institute

"长子口"方尊

西周
鹿邑长子口墓出土
高37.9厘米
河南省文物考古研究所藏
Square bronze Zun inscribed "Zhangzikou"
Western Zhou Dynasty
Excavated from the tomb of Zhangzikou in Luyi County
Height:37.9cm
Collected in Henan Archeology and Cultural Relics Research Institute

104 礼乐大成 赫赫成周

"长子口" 四耳簋

西周
鹿邑长子口墓出土
高 14.4 厘米
河南省文物考古研究所藏
Bronze Gui inscribed "Zhangzikou"
Western Zhou Dynasty
Excavated from the tomb of Zhangzikou in Luyi County
Height: 14.4cm
Collected in Henan Archeology and Cultural Relics Research Institute

火纹罍

西周
鹿邑长子口墓出土
高29厘米　口径15厘米
河南省文物考古研究所藏
Bronze Lei with flame motif
Western Zhou Dynasty
Excavated from the tomb of Zhangzikou in Luyi County
Height:29cm Mouth:15cm
Collected in Henan Archeology and Cultural Relics Research Institute

108 礼乐大成 赫赫成周

云雷纹盉

西周
鹿邑长子口墓出土
高 27.6 厘米 口径 10.6 厘米
河南省文物考古研究所藏
Bronze He with cloud and thunder motif
Western Zhou Dynasty
Excavated from the tomb of "Zhangzikou" in Luyi County
Height:27.6cm Mouth:10.6cm
Collected in Henan Archeology and Cultural Relics Research Institute

云雷纹尊

西周
鹿邑长子口墓出土
高 25.2 厘米
河南省文物考古研究所藏
Bronze Zun with cloud and thunder motif
Western Zhou Dynasty
Excavated from the tomb of Zhangzikou in Luyi County
Height:25.2cm
Collected in Henan Archeology and Cultural Relics Research Institute

兽面纹觥

西周
鹿邑长子口墓出土
高 21.4 厘米
河南省文物考古研究所藏
Bronze Gong with beast-mask motif
Western Zhou Dynasty
Excavated from the tomb of Zhangzikou in Luyi County
Height: 21.4cm
Collected in Henan Archeology and Cultural Relics Research Institute

兽面纹鼎

西周
鹿邑长子口墓出土
高19厘米
河南省文物考古研究所藏
Bronze Ding with beast-mask motif
Western Zhou Dynasty
Excavated from the tomb of Zhangzikou in Luyi County
Height:19cm
Collected in Henan Archeology and Cultural Relics Research Institute

郑州洼刘舌族青铜器

舌族是商周时期在政治、经济、文化及军事上都占有相当重要地位的国族。商末周初时期，舌族主要活动于今郑州、荥阳之间。之后，舌族被迫迁移至鹤壁一带，但依然活跃于西周的政治舞台上；直至西周中期以后，其地位大大削弱，不仅没有相关铜器出土，甚至在先秦文献中都难觅其踪。

"舌"戈

西周
1993年郑州黄河大观采集
长24.3厘米
郑州博物馆藏
Bronze Ge inscribed "She"
Western Zhou Dynasty
Gathered from the Yellow River Grand View, Zhengzhou, 1993
Length: 24.3cm
Collected in Zhengzhou Museum

"舌"卣

西周
1999年郑州洼刘出土
高38.5厘米
郑州博物馆藏
Bronze You inscribed "She"
Western Zhou Dynasty
Excavated from Waliu, Zhengzhou, 1999
Height:38.5cm
Collected in Zhengzhou Museum

　　卣呈扁圆体，深腹下垂，下腹圆鼓，低圈足，提梁两端兽首与卣颈两侧半圆环系套合，盖面中间突立四面人首状钮。卣体外饰有互相垂直对称的四条扉棱；提梁上面饰两组双体夔龙纹；盖与卣腹各饰四组凤纹，卣颈部与圈足部均饰四组凤纹。卣盖与器底均铸有铭文，其中有一"舌"字。

兽面纹鼎

西周
1999年郑州洼刘出土
高30厘米
郑州博物馆藏
Bronze Ding with beast-mask pattern
Western Zhou Dynasty
Excavated from Waliu, Zhengzhou, 1999
Height: 30cm
Collected in Zhengzhou Museum

"舌韦亚"爵

西周
1993年郑州黄河大观采集
高18.5厘米
郑州博物馆藏
Bronze Jue inscribed "She Wei Ya"
Western Zhou Dynasty
Gathered from the Yellow River Grand View, Zhengzhou, 1993
Height:18.5cm
Collected in Zhengzhou Museum

平顶山应国贵族青铜器

据甲骨卜辞记载，商代已有应国。周初成王改封其弟于应，至公元前七世纪初为楚所灭，立国约 350 年。应都地望在今河南平顶山滍阳镇一带。平顶山应国贵族墓地的考古发现，揭示了这一湮灭已久的中原古国文化面貌。所出器物不仅工艺精湛，而且青铜器铭文内容对于考证应侯世系、应国职官、礼仪制度及应与周边诸侯国的关系均具有重要史料价值。

应国国君周武王之子应叔之墓发掘现场

平顶山应国墓地 M50 铜器出土现场照片

应侯"再"盨

西周
平顶山应国墓地出土
高 22.4 厘米
河南省文物考古研究所藏
Bronze Xu inscribed "Cheng", the prince of Ying State
Western Zhou Dynasty
Excavated from the necropolis of Ying State in Pingdingshan City
Height:22.4cm
Collected in Henan Archeology and Cultural Relics Research Institute

瓦纹匜

西周
平顶山应国墓地出土
长 32.3 厘米
河南省文物考古研究所藏
Bronze Yi with tile motif
Western Zhou Dynasty
Excavated from the necropolis of Ying State in Pingdingshan City
Length:32.3cm
Collected in Henan Archeology and Cultural Relics Research Institute

垂鳞纹鼎

西周
平顶山应国墓地出土
高 26 厘米
河南省文物考古研究所藏
Bronze Ding with scale motif
Western Zhou Dynasty
Excavated from the necropolis of Ying State in Pingdingshan City
Height:26cm
Collected in Henan Archeology and Cultural Relics Research Institute

侧人面像

西周

侧人面像

西周
平顶山应国墓地出土

正人面像

西周
平顶山应国墓地出土
高15厘米
河南省文物考古研究所藏
Bronze mask
Western Zhou Dynasty
Excavated from the necropolis of Ying State in Pingdingshan City
Height:15cm
Collected in Henan Archeology and Cultural Relics Research Institute

正人面像

西周
平顶山应国墓地出土
高 15.7 厘米
河南省文物考古研究所藏
Bronze mask
Western Zhou Dynasty
Excavated from the necropolis of Ying State in Pingdingshan City
Height:15.7cm
Collected in Henan Archeology and Cultural Relics Research Institute

三门峡虢国贵族青铜器

周初封文王之弟虢仲、虢叔于东、西二虢。东虢在今河南荥阳,春秋初年为郑所灭;西虢在今陕西宝鸡,西周末年迁至河南三门峡及山西平陆一带,公元前655年,为晋所灭。虢国墓地位于今三门峡市北黄河南岸,20世纪50年代以来,共发现数百座墓葬,排列有序,等级分明,再现了周王朝分封制下诸侯国君及其家族的丧葬礼制。

虢国墓地 M2001 青铜器出土现场

138 礼乐大成 赫赫成周

"丰白"簠

西周
1991年三门峡虢国墓M2006出土
高21.6厘米
三门峡市虢国博物馆藏
Bronze Fu inscribed "Feng Bo"
Western Zhou Dynasty
Excavated from the No.2006 tomb of Guo State in Shanmenxia City
Height:21.6cm
Collected in Guo State Museum

  器与盖形制、纹饰、尺寸均相同。腹壁斜直，腹两侧有兽首耳，矩形圈足，四边正中有缺。腹中部饰双首曲体夔龙纹，沿下及圈足饰窃曲纹，盖顶、器底饰连体蟠夔纹，中心兽目突起。器、盖对铭，共3行14字（重文2个），依器铭行款释为：

  丰白（伯）盄（叔）父
  乍（作）匡（簠）其子子
  孙孙永宝用

兽目交连纹鼎

西周
虢国墓地出土
高 37.3 厘米
三门峡市虢国博物馆藏
Bronze Ding with beast-eye motif
Western Zhou Dynasty
Excavated from the necropolis of Guo State in Shanmenxia City
Height:37.3cm
Collected in Guo State Museum

兽面纹鬲

西周
虢国墓地出土
高 13.5 厘米
三门峡市虢国博物馆藏
Bronze Li with beast-mask motif
Western Zhou Dynasty
Excavated from the necropolis of Guo State in Shanmenxia City
Height:13.5cm
Collected in Guo State Museum

144 礼乐大成 赫赫成周

波带纹方甗

西周
虢国墓地出土
高 42.5 厘米
三门峡市虢国博物馆藏
Bronze Yan with wave motif
Western Zhou Dynasty
Excavated from the necropolis of Guo State in Shanmenxia City
Height:42.5cm
Collected in Guo State Museum

兽目交连纹盘

西周
虢国墓地出土
高 17.5 厘米　口径 41.8 厘米
三门峡市虢国博物馆藏
Bronze plate with beast-eye motif
Western Zhou Dynasty
Excavated from the necropolis of Guo State in Shanmenxia City
Height:17.5cm Mouth:41.8cm
Collected in Guo State Museum

瓦纹匜

西周
虢国墓地出土
长32厘米
三门峡市虢国博物馆藏
Bronze Yi with tile motif
Western Zhou Dynasty
Excavated from the necropolis of Guo State in Shanmenxia City
Length:32cm
Collected in Guo State Museum

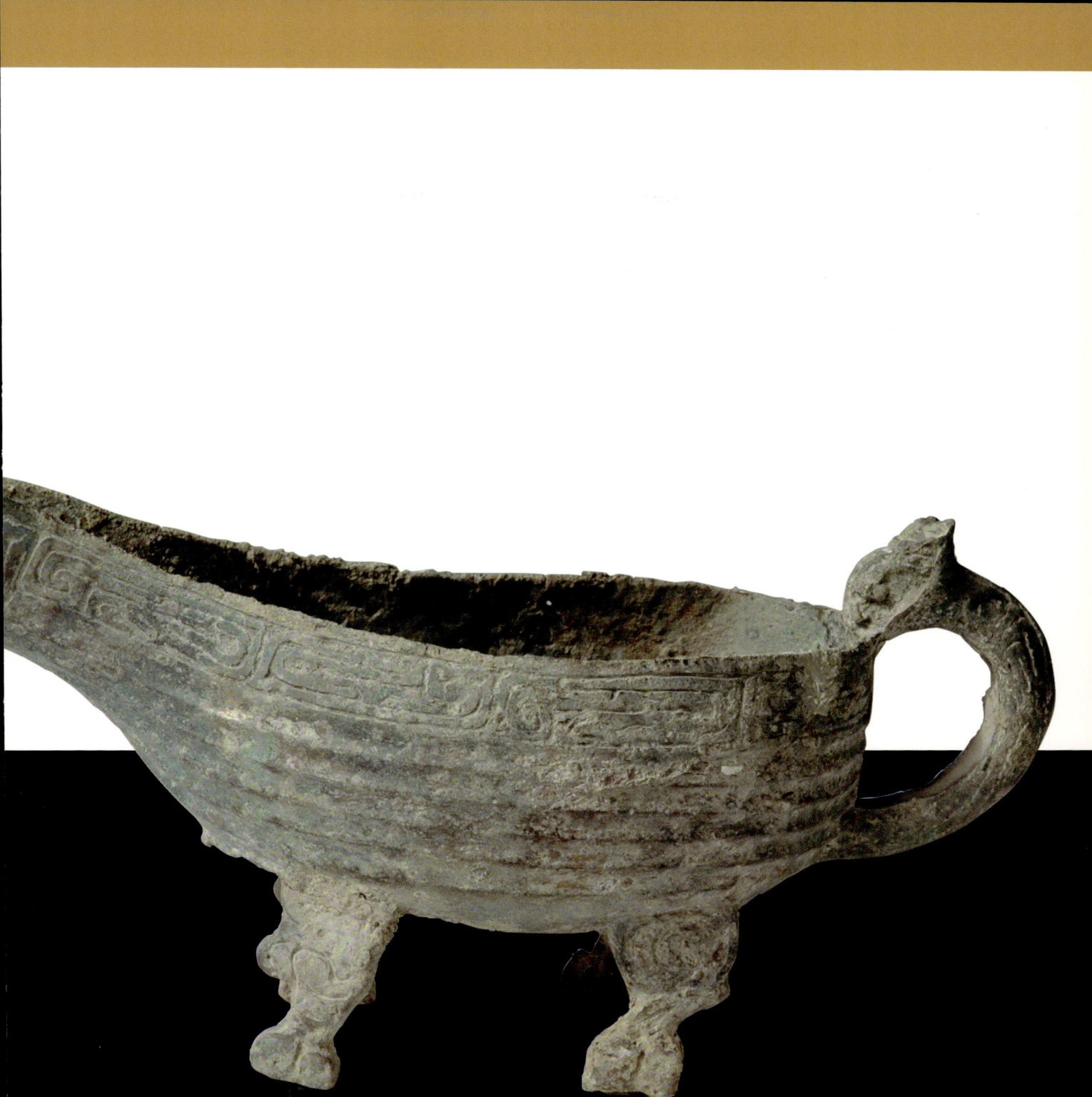

兽目交连纹壶

西周
虢国墓地出土
高 39 厘米
三门峡市虢国博物馆藏
Bronze pot with beast-eye motif
Western Zhou Dynasty
Excavated from the necropolis of Guo State in Shanmenxia City
Height:39cm
Collected in Guo State Museum

"父乙"角

西周
信阳浉河港出土
高 28 厘米
信阳博物馆藏

Bronze Jiao inscribed "Fu Yi"
Western Zhou Dynasty
Excavated from Shihe Port in Xinyang City
Height:28cm
Collected in Xinyang Museum

　　通体呈深浓闪亮的墨绿色，折沿、直腹、三角棱形足、有盖，用斜子母扣扣合。头顶饰桥形钮，还有扉棱和饕餮纹，云雷纹衬底，腹饰扉棱和饕餮纹，云雷纹衬底，钣饰兽首纹，足外饰蕉叶蝉纹，盖内和腹内各有一组铭文，三行十二字："晨肇贮宝作父乙用？尊彝，毁？册"，"晨肇贮"是作器人，墓主人"乙"是其父，此器应是"晨肇贮"为亡父所作的祭器，其构思巧妙，瑰丽庄重，是我国考古发现青铜角最大者之一，考古界称之为"角王"。

群雄逐鹿 异彩纷呈 第四部分
东周时期（公元前770年～前221年）

自公元前770年周平王东迁洛阳，开始了历史上所称的东周时期。"周失其鹿，天下共逐之"，中原成为列国逐鹿争霸的大战场。这一时期王室衰微、列国蜂起、诸侯争霸，新兴势力不断出现，意识形态领域空前活跃，文化由于创新与个性变得纷繁多彩。青铜器作为这一时代风貌的"物化"反映，造型由厚重威严变得奇巧轻灵，浓厚的神秘色彩渐渐消退，纹饰开始变得更接近于生活。

Part Ⅳ Eastern Zhou Dynasty (770 B.C.~221 B.C.)
Since King Ping of Zhou Dynasty moved capital to Luoyang at 770 B.C., started the history of the Eastern Zhou Dynasty . The Central Plains became a big battlefield where the different states competed against the hegemony of China. In this period the Zhou royal waned in influence, the states rose up and contend for hegemony, and new powers appeared constantly, the field of ideology was more active than ever, the culture became variety that due to innovation and individuality. Bronzes as reflection of "materialized ", that the styling of bronze ware varied from heavy to light, the strong mystery faded away gradually, the ornamentation in bronzes become more close to life.

洛阳东周王室青铜器

春秋战国时期洛阳作为天子之都,在星罗棋布的列国都邑中,仍保持着宗主国的躯壳,是列国都城中规格最高的都城之一。这里出土青铜器数量巨大,集中分布在东周王城及东周王陵区。早在民国年间,金村陵区就出土众多极为精美的青铜器,让世人震惊。这些青铜器除铸有各种精美的蟠螭纹外,还出现了人与虎、豹、鹿等兽搏斗场面的狩猎纹图案,特别是错金银青铜器的大量发现及浑铸、焊接、熔铸等工艺的运用,标志着东周时期青铜铸造仍处在一个比较发达的阶段。

"天子驾六"车马坑

东周王城平面图

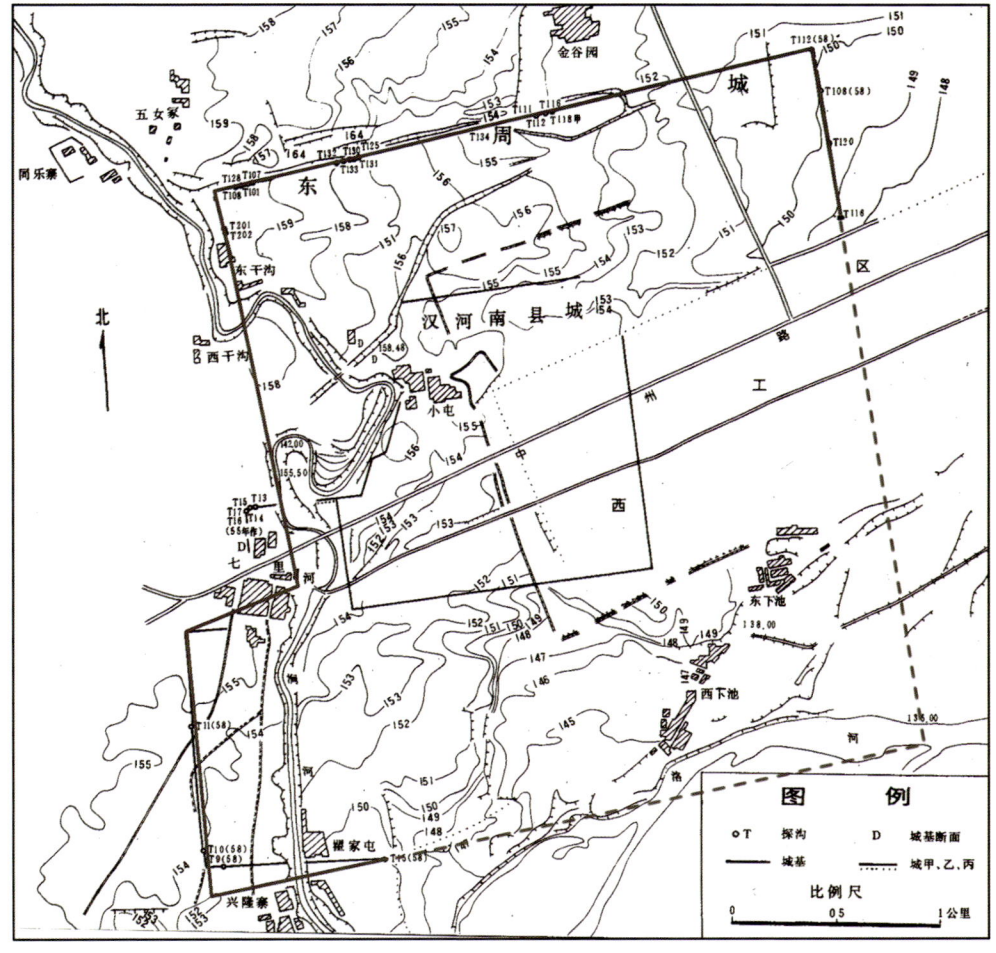

158 群雄逐鹿 异彩纷呈

跽坐人形灯座

战国
洛阳解放路出土
高 14.4 厘米
洛阳博物馆藏
Bronze lamp-base Figurine on Knees
Warring States Period
Excavated from Jiefang Road in Luoyang City
Height: 14.4cm
Collected in Luoyang Museum

乳丁纹壶

战国
洛阳解放路出土
高 35.5 厘米
洛阳博物馆藏
Bronze pot with nipples motif
Warring States Period
Excavated from Jiefang road, Luoyang City
Height: 35.5cm
Collected in Luoyang Museum

162 群雄逐鹿 异彩纷呈

透雕四龙纹方镜

战国
洛阳西工区出土
边长 11 厘米
洛阳博物馆藏
Square bronze mirror with four-dragon in openwork
Warring States Period
Excavated from Xigong District, Luoyang City
Length: 11cm
Collected in Luoyang Museum

嵌玻璃珠"山"纹镜

战国
洛阳西工区出土
直径14.5cm
洛阳博物馆藏
Bronze mirror with patterns of characters "Shan" and inlaid with glass beads
Warring States Period
Excavated from Xigong District, Luoyang City
Diameter: 14.5cm
Collected in Luoyang Museum

错金嵌绿松石龙形带钩

战国
洛阳西工区出土
长 21.6cm
洛阳博物馆藏
Bronze belt hook inlaid with gold and turquoise
Warring States Period
Excavated from Xigong District, Luoyang City
Length: 21.6cm
Collected in Luoyang Museum

错金鸭形带钩

战国
洛阳手表厂出土
长 7.7 厘米
洛阳博物馆藏
Bronze duck-shaped belt hook
Warring States Period
Excavated from Luoyang City
Length:7.7cm
Collected in Luoyang Museum

新郑郑国青铜器

公元前806年,周宣王封其弟姬友于郑(今陕西省华县)。周平王东迁,郑国也迁到洛阳以东,并灭虢国、郐国,在此建都,取名新郑。中原的郑国,地处列国间频繁的交往,会盟、征战、婚媾、商贸等中心,经济文化先进,人民富足多识。春秋之际,郑文化在礼乐上挑战传统,开辟了列国文化的崭新面貌。

蟠螭纹鼎（9件）

高 47～55.2 厘米
Height:47～55.2cm

蟠螭纹簋（8件）

高 20.7～22.7 厘米
Height:20.7～22.7cm

蟠螭纹鬲（9件）

高 12.1～12.2 厘米
Height:12.1～12.2cm

春秋
新郑出土
河南省文物考古研究所藏
Bronze Li with interlaced-hydras motif(a group of nine)
Spring and Autumn Period
Excavated from Xinzheng City
Collected in Henan Archeology and Cultural Relics Research Institute

1993年以来，在郑韩故城的东城发现的郑国社稷祭祀遗存，排列有多座青铜礼乐器坑和殉马坑，并遗存有同时期的夯筑围墙墙基。较为完整的青铜礼器和青铜乐器组合特征，填补了周代祭祀礼制形式的空白，对于研究当时祭礼的用鼎、用牲和与之有关的仪礼具体运作有重要意义。特别是九鼎八簋的礼器组合打破了周礼的规制，表现了东周礼崩乐坏的社会现象。

龙纹方壶

春秋
新郑出土
高 65.6 厘米
河南省文物考古研究所藏
Square bronze pot with dragon motif
Spring and Autumn Period
Excavated from Xinzheng City
Height:65.6cm
Collected in Henan Archeology and Cultural Relics Research Institute

蟠螭纹圆壶

春秋
新郑出土
高 33.9 厘米
河南省文物考古研究所藏
Round bronze pot with interlaced-hydras motif
Spring and Autumn Period
Excavated from Xinzheng City
Height:33.9cm
Collected in Henan Archeology and Cultural Relics Research Institute

龙纹豆

春秋
新郑出土
高 19.4 厘米
河南省文物考古研究所藏
Bronze Dou with dragon motif
Spring and Autumn Period
Excavated from Xinzheng City
Height:19.4cm
Collected in Henan Archeology and Cultural Relics Research Institute

弦纹鉴

春秋
新郑出土
高 16.8 厘米
河南省文物考古研究所藏
Bronze Jian with bow string motif
Spring and Autumn Period
Excavated from Xinzheng City
Height:16.8cm
Collected in Henan Archeology and Cultural Relics Research Institute

淅川楚国青铜器

楚立国周初，僻居江汉蛮荒之地，"筚路蓝缕，以启山林"，从周成王封熊绎开始，至春秋楚庄王时，国力日盛。楚人数百年间一直致力于北上中原，图霸诸夏，原本属于周文化范畴的汉淮诸姬和南国诸侯，都在楚人北上、东渐的过程中，归附于楚而最终为其所灭。楚拓地千里，陈兵周郊，问鼎中原，表现出称霸天下的雄心。

徐家岭9号墓发掘全景

"王子午"鼎

春秋
淅川下寺楚墓出土
高 15.7 厘米
河南省文物考古研究所藏
Bronze Ding inscribed "Wang Zi Wu"
Spring and Autumn Period
Excavated from Xichuan County
Height:15.7cm
Collected in Henan Archeology and Cultural Relics Research Institute

　　器内壁及底部有铭文 14 行 84 字。铭文表达了对先祖的追思,叙说王子午自己施德政于民的业绩,并教育子孙须以此为准则。"王子午"即文献所载楚庄王之子,字子庚,楚康王时为令尹。为问鼎中原的春秋霸主楚庄王第五子,楚康王时为楚国令尹(相当于丞相)。王子午鼎共出 7 件,形制相同,大小相次。整组器物造型雄伟,制作精良,装饰繁缛,精细华美,且多处使用了焊接工艺,显示出春秋晚期楚国青铜铸造技术的高超水平,表现出楚国青铜器的崭新风貌。

国王与诸侯—中国河南青铜文明 *183*

184 群雄逐鹿 异彩纷呈

镶嵌绿松石神兽

春秋
淅川徐家岭出土
高 48 厘米
河南省文物考古研究所藏
The mythological animal-shaped object inlaid with turquoise
Spring and Autumn Period
Excavated from Xichuan County
Height:48cm
Collected in Henan Archeology and Cultural Relics Research Institute

　　是出于河南淅川徐家岭九号墓的一对神兽之一。主体龙首，虎身，龟足，头上以六条蜿蜒纠绕的小龙构成兽角，背部曲形架上立一同样形态的龙形奔兽，遍布全身的龙凤纹饰，以翠绿色的孔雀石镶嵌而成。而背上与腹下的钮与方形的插孔，证明这对神兽是一种乐器的器架。

186 群雄逐鹿 异彩纷呈

多戈戟

战国
新蔡葛岭出土
高 14.1 厘米
河南省文物考古研究所藏
Bronze Ji, the halberd
Warring States Period
Excavated from Xincai County
Height: 14.1cm
Collected in Henan Archeology and Cultural Relics Research Institute

兽面纹盉

战国
信阳市平桥区城阳出土
高 34 厘米
信阳博物馆藏

Bronze He with beast-mask motif
Warring States Period
Excavated from Pingqiao District, Xinyang City
Height: 34cm
Collected in Xinyang Museum

国王与诸侯—中国河南青铜文明 *189*

190 群雄逐鹿 异彩纷呈

镂空盆形器

战国
信阳市平桥区城阳出土
高 13 厘米　口径 24 厘米
信阳博物馆藏
Basin-shaped bronze object in openwork
Warring States Period
Excavated from Pingqiao District, Xinyang City
Height: 13cm　Mouth: 24cm
Collected in Xinyang Museum

淮诸小国青铜器

汉淮地区处中原与荆楚之间，历来是上古民族交错杂居之地，既有复杂的历史渊源，又有错综的文化形态。周初在此地分封了许多同姓和异姓诸侯，以作为王室的南土屏障。在东周长期的列国兼并争霸中，诸小国纷纷为强国吞并，只留下这些小国墓葬所出风格各异的青铜器，述说一段缤纷的故国往事。

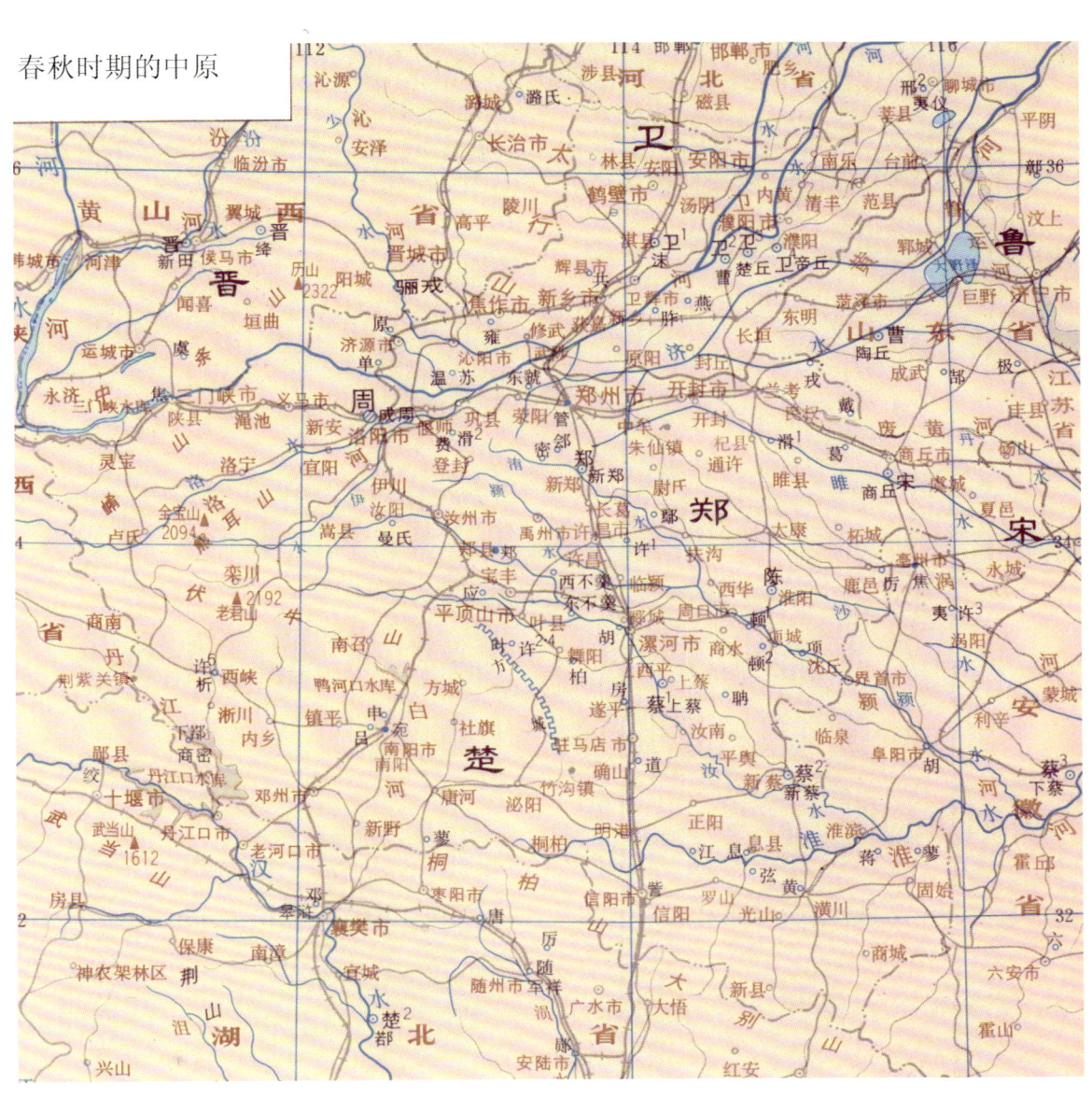

春秋时期的中原

194 群雄逐鹿 异彩纷呈

"黄君孟"鼎

春秋
光山宝相寺出土
高 27 厘米
河南博物院藏

Bronze Ding inscribed "Huang Jun Meng"
Spring and Autumn Period
Excavated from Baoxiang Temple in Guangshan County
Height: 27cm
Collected in Henan Museum

"黄夫人"豆

春秋
光山宝相寺出土
高 29 厘米
信阳博物馆藏
Bronze Dou inscribed "Madam Huang"
Spring and Autumn Period
Excavated from Baoxiang Temple in Guangshan County
Height:29cm
Collected in Xinyang Museum

198 群雄逐鹿 异彩纷呈

"黄夫人"壶

春秋
光山宝相寺出土
高 30.7 厘米
信阳博物馆藏
Bronze pot inscribed "Madam Huang"
Spring and Autumn Period
Excavated from Baoxiang Temple in Guangshan County
Height: 30.7cm
Collected in Xinyang Museum

"番君"盘

春秋
潢川刘砦出土
高14.8厘米 口径34.9厘米
信阳博物馆藏
Bronze plate inscribed "Fan Jun"
Spring and Autumn Period
Excavated from Huangchuan County
Height:14.8cm Mouth:34.9cm
Collected in Xinyang Museum

牺尊

春秋
信阳市平西村出土
高 14.7 厘米
信阳博物馆藏
Beast-shpaed bronze Zun
Spring and Autumn Period
Excavated from Pingxi Village, Xinyang City

镶红铜龙纹方豆

春秋
固始侯古堆出土
高 29.3 厘米
河南博物院藏
Bronze Dou inlaid with copper
Spring and Autumn Period
Excavated from Pingxi Village, Xinyang City
Height: 29.3cm
Collected in Henan Museum

几何纹壶

战国
淮滨王岗乡出土
高 36 厘米
信阳博物馆藏
Bronze pot with geometry motif
Warring States Period
Excavated from Huaibin County, Xinyang City
Height: 36cm
Collected in Xinyang Museum

铜鼎

春秋
上蔡郭庄1号墓出土
通高88厘米 口径79厘米
信阳博物馆藏
Bronze Ding with geometry motif
Warring States Period
Excavated from the NO.1 tomb in Guozhuang, Shangcai Country
Height:88cm Mouth:79cm
Collected in Xinyang Museum

结 语

中原的历史,是中华民族历史的缩影。

中原百姓的心路,是中华民族魂灵之形成轨迹。

中原文化的创造者,同样是中华民族文明的缔造者。

Conclusion

The history of the Central Plains, is the epitome of the Chinese nation history.
The soul course of the people of the Central Plains , is the process of the soul of the Chinese nation .
The creators of the culture of the Central Plains , are also the creators of the civilization of the Chinese nation.

《国王与诸侯 — 中国河南青铜文明》

撰 稿 人：李 琴　谢虎军　高西省

翻　　译：王军花　王游美　赵曦萌

摄　　影：牛爱红　祝 贺　阮 超
　　　　　陈 巍　张立新　常 军
　　　　　谷 波　陈金龙

责任校对：高西省　王军花　赵星汉

封面设计：孙永明　李 岩

装帧设计：张 波　吕建明

版式设计：孙永明　石 越

插图处理：苏 钰　徐阳光　聂荣倩